21 Days to Die

*The Canadian Guide to
End of Life*

Linda Hochstetler
MSW, RSW

21 Days to Die
Linda Hochstetler
Text © Linda Hochstetler, 2021
All rights reserved

Cover photo: AliCris, Shutterstock
Author photo: Kristina Ruddick
Editing & Design: John H. Negru

a
greenbank
book

Published by
The Sumeru Press Inc.
Manotick, ON
Canada

ISBN 978-1-896559-72-8 (pbk.).

LIBRARY AND ARCHIVES CANADA CATALOGUING IN PUBLICATION

Title: 21 days to die : the Canadian guide to end of life / Linda Hochstetler, MSW, RSW.
Other titles: Twenty-one days to die | Canadian guide to end of life
Names: Hochstetler, Linda, author.
Description: A Greenbank Book. | Includes bibliographical references.
Identifiers: Canadiana 20210226331 | ISBN 9781896559728 (softcover)
Subjects: LCSH: Terminal care. | LCSH: Death. | LCSH: Palliative treatment. | LCSH: Hospice care. |
  LCSH: Grief.
Classification: LCC R726.8 .H63 2021 | DDC 616.02/9—dc23

For more information about Greenbank Books and The Sumeru Press visit us at *www.sumeru-books.com*

Contents

Introduction

What would it be like if you recognized that you had only 21 days left to live? Would you make any different decisions? Would your values be any different? Would you want anything different from the people around you? Can you imagine the fearlessness it takes to look death in the face, knowing you have only 21 days left to live?

For most people with advancing diseases, there are signs that death will be soon. Diseases have many trajectories, but at a certain stage, the ceasing of life becomes certain. At 21 days, there are usually no more treatment options with any real promise of quality of life. At 21 days, there is usually no chance of recovery or reprieve.

21 days is not the precise number of days to recognize all deaths, and I do not mean to imply that death can be managed or needs to be predicted precisely. Death is a mystery, and we don't want to take all of the mystery away. However, there are a number of signs of impending death and they follow in a predictable sequence. I write this book in the hope that all Canadians will come to recognize these signs. Together we can share this information and be ready to welcome death when the time is right.

@

I was initiated into a direct experience of death in 1986 at the age of 22. I had just recently started dating a young man about a month prior. The relationship hadn't really even gotten off the ground, with no long-term dreams or fantasies yet. Then, while riding his bicycle, he was hit by a truck and died instantly. I attended his funeral, which was the first home funeral I'd ever attended. He was buried in a homemade pine casket in the purple tie-dyed T-shirt that we'd made together the week before. I sat with friends and family and that pine casket in the living room of his parents' house and said goodbye to my innocence and to my ignorance of death. Gone. I moved on and soon met my first husband, but I had unwittingly joined the club. The club that knows at a very deep level that death happens. It's real.

A few years later, I attended school and trained to become a social worker. The first 20 years of my social work career involved a lot of death training. I often spoke with people after a sudden death. Maybe a workplace accident. Maybe a suicide or homicide. Or maybe a sudden medical event that ended a life. Often, I was the grief counsellor brought in to talk to the people left behind, usually work colleagues. And for almost all of these events, no one, including the person who died, saw it coming. Certainly, their work colleagues and managers never saw it coming. There was a lot of fast adjusting to do for everyone. The shock and surprise on the faces were often painful for me to see and hold. It was as if they had never considered the thought of death coming into the workplace. These encounters helped reveal a deep level of denial of death all around me. People struggled to handle death, as if they had had no preparation for it.

How different would it be if we could see death coming? Would that make it any easier? Easier for the dying person? Easier for their family and friends? And what could we do to make that change?

Around this time, I found myself talking to people about death as if it were a normal part of life, and I began noticing how they seemed to be shocked to hear this – as if they had never let themselves think about death under any circumstances. Like death was a surprise. A part of life that they had never been told about. I know that sometimes a particular death is a surprise. But death as a concept is a surprise? That death happens is a surprise? It baffled me.

@

I have always tried to live a meaningful life. This includes actively assessing my own values and knowing which values matter most to me at any given time. I haven't always been known as "the Death Lady", as I have been called on numerous occasions. Once, when I was walking down Roncesvalles Avenue near my home in Toronto, and a stranger whom I've never met did a rubberneck to look at me and shouted, "Hey, you're the Death Lady!". They walked on, and I had no idea who they were or what they knew about me, but I am ok with that nickname.

Following the death of my boyfriend, I was too young to really notice the shift in realization that had happened. I never attended grief counselling and only talked about it for a few weeks with friends and family around the funeral itself. Mostly I moved on. It's only in hindsight that I can see the influence this experience had on my view of life. And of death. At a visceral level, I recognized that no one lives forever. Death comes, whether we're ready for it or not.

When I turned 50, and tipped over undeniably into the second half of my life, my interest in death sparked for real. My willingness to step further into the fire just happened. I began thinking about what legacy I wanted to leave for the planet. I began thinking about how to leave an imprint that was more than just a child, a continuation of my DNA. I accepted that up to this point I hadn't really done enough to justify my time on the planet. I committed to changing this, and began thinking about what small change I could make that might live on beyond my own death.

Thinking about death and legacy wasn't a huge detour for me. I was trained as a social worker and psychotherapist, and had specialized in delivering grief support to workplaces following critical incidents, often fatalities in the workplace related to workplace accidents, suicides, or fear of death following a bank robbery. However, this early work was more about bringing employees together to talk about their reactions and encouraging leaders to show both compassion and competence towards their employees during those tough times.

My new interest became more about helping others face death long before it happened to them. As I looked around, it became apparent to me that Canadians avoid talking about death under any circumstances. When death does happen, it catches people off guard. No one seems to have any language for talking about death. We have all heard many euphemisms to describe a death – passing, losing a loved one, and even sleeping. No wonder we have children afraid of doing well at school (in case they might "pass," too) or going to bed (and "sleeping" like granny).

I read many books about death. I noticed that whenever people wrote about death, they focused mostly on the dying part, but called it a book about death. I began clearly differentiating between thinking about the dying process, and thinking about death. And I noticed that the English language uses a strange sequence in referring to the end of life as death and dying – this sequence is backwards. It may sound bumpy at first, but I have committed to follow the correct chronology and refer to this as dying and death (rather than death and dying). You will see it referred to as dying and death throughout this book.

℗

And I began listening to whoever was talking about death. There wasn't a lot out there of this, even as recently as 2014! The first group I did find was the Death Café movement.[1] This public education movement was founded in England in 2011 by Jon Underwood and Sue Barsky Reid (Jon's mother). They based their model on the ideas of Bernard Crettaz, the Swiss sociologist and ethnologist who set up the Café Mortel to talk about death.[2] They noted that death is an uncomfortable topic to discuss, and that death denial is common in societies around the world. They wondered whether accepting death might mean that people find more purpose and meaning in their lives, that remembering death is coming for us might help us live more fully, joyfully, and consciously. They created a model of gathering people together in public settings, like cafés, and having thoughtful, respectful, and engaging conversations about dying and death. They set guidelines limiting sales (products or services) and promotion of particular ideas. Instead, they insist that gatherings

---

1   Death Café. deathcafe.com

2   Full Interview with Jon Underwood and Bernard Crettaz. (December 8, 2014). youtube.com/watch?v=3lDtmJyvu2k

be neutral and have no pre-set agendas. Their model has grown in popularity, and as of February, 2021, there have been more than 12,000+ Death Cafés hosted in 75 countries around the world.[3]

Sadly, Jon Underwood died at the age of 44 in 2018. He left behind a wife and kids, and a whole movement helping people think about death before its time. I'm happy to say his Death Café model continues on. People continue to want to talk about death, and I am told time and time again that there is nowhere else to do so. The dinner table is off limits to death. Party conversations avoid any mention of death. Most people would rather talk about superficial topics, and certainly not death.

I needed to get a feel for the movement myself. For my first Death Café, I drove for an hour in a snowstorm to a sleepy suburb north of Toronto to sit with 12 other people and talk about death. We gathered in a cheery coffee shop, settled in with delicious pastries and tea, and looked around nervously at each other. I noted that in this group it was mostly white people around my own age. The place was abandoned at 7 p.m. that night, except for us, and it was eerily quiet as we waited for the session to begin. I don't remember much about that first meeting, except that I felt at home there. I felt I was surrounded by other weirdoes like myself who had many stories they wanted to share about death. I also remember that we laughed a lot, no one cried, and the feelings weren't even very sombre. We shared an instant intimacy, earned in the sharing of a secret death story that we didn't often get to share.

After another such evening at a Death Café in Toronto, I felt I was ready to host one myself. I turned to my local coffee shop/pub – The Belljar Café (since closed) – to help me out. The co-owner, Lisa Kannako, had recently hosted my 50th birthday party, and she was more than happy to offer the space for free and to host my group. I took it for granted that she would agree, but it was only later, when I began looking for a second location in Brampton and got turned down by more than 20 places, that I realized how lucky I had been with my first venue.

> When Linda approached me asking if she could run a regular meeting at my café, the Belljar, explaining that the purpose would be to discuss death – I said yes right from the start. I had known Linda from the day we opened our doors, and she was always warm-hearted and inclusive. I trusted that whatever she wanted to do in our space would be meaningful and important. Death is a topic never discussed yet inevitably present in our lives. It affects those we love and leave behind, for years beyond the event itself, sometimes becoming a painful burden, so steps to processing this major life event with others seemed like an opportunity for acceptance. I was very curious to see how it would be approached in an open group session.

---

3 Death Café. deathcafe.com

Death seems like an internal and personal event, yet it comes to each of us, so there must be universal aspects of the experience. As I witnessed groups of people come into the cafe month after month, sitting in groups talking, it was incredibly peaceful and I felt it to be rewarding to everyone who showed up. Just to be willing to talk about something so outside of our daily existence even made it more essential. Talking about something brings it out into the light, normalizes it; removing the dark, the fear, changes it completely. Moving on with life, to be fully here, is the best thing we can do for ourselves and those who love, and have loved, us. I'm glad to have provided a safe inclusive space for this important work.

Lisa Kannako, Co-owner of Belljar Café

In 2015, I began hosting my own Death Cafés. The first one drew 30 participants, and since then I have hosted 23 Death Cafés in four different locations around the Greater Toronto Area, drawing over more than 800 participants. Whenever I contemplate stopping organizing them, participants beg me to continue. My most recent Death Café, a Zoom online event in the midst of what's otherwise known as serious Zoom fatigue, brought out our largest number ever – 42 participants.

For anyone who is curious about Death Cafés, and want to find out more about what happens at them first, I highly recommend listening to the story about this. A producer from a popular CBC Radio talk show – The Current – attended one of the early Death Cafés and aired a show about it.[4] There is even an interview with Jon Underwood before he died. It clearly reports that people tend to talk as much about living fully as about death.

On any given night, I help arrange the 20-42 participants into small groups of four or five. There are always a few young people still in their 20s, plus a few older people in their 60s and 70s, but most are in their 40s and 50s. Participants come from all walks of life, all backgrounds, all races, looking like a snapshot of Toronto. Some work in death professions (like funeral home workers, death doulas, and grief counsellors), but the majority are ordinary Canadians just wanting to explore death. Some come saying they have experienced a recent death, sharing both positive and negative experiences. It is common for them to say they just want to talk about death and aren't looking for grief therapy at all.

In April, 2018, I presented a paper to the annual Ontario Hospice Palliative Care Conference on the topic of Death Cafés and their alignment with hospice palliative care principles. It was a standing-room-only presentation that packed the large hotel room. Attendees asked questions about how to host Death Cafés of their own around the province.

At each Death Café, I speak at the beginning to set the stage by introducing

---

4 CBC Radio (May 12, 2016). *Death Cafes Serve Up Life and Death Conversations.*

myself and giving a history of the movement. When we meet in person, participants are sitting in small groups around small tables. For online groups, we divide into Breakout rooms. I invite the participants to introduce themselves by first name and to say why they came. After that I direct them to ask questions or to tell their personal stories about death, and let it go from there. I give no further direction or limitation, other than being respectful of all viewpoints expressed. There are often titters and nervous laughter initially as everyone chooses their first small group, but within a few minutes they settle down. Halfway through the evening, I encourage mixing up tables and sitting with a new small group, to provide a variety of experiences. Every night is different. I float around listening in on the various conversations. People have always been respectful, and there is never silence at any table. People leave telling me that it has been a long time since they have had such a meaningful conversation with strangers.

A large number of artists have attended through the years, and often they have been working on a film or an art instalment related to death. I have been invited to participate in numerous podcasts, documentary films, and other art and media forms dealing with dying and death over the years. A Death Café is a useful step on their journey to explore an idea related to death.

There are regulars who have attended most of the Death Cafés for several years. Many people drop in and out, depending on what's happening in their own lives. Each time, first timers comprise about half of the group.

> It was the sense that I was not fully alive that drew me to be interested in death. I thought that if I were able to fully imagine my own death, that it would awaken in me the perspective that I was missing to understand the value of my life. Not feeling fully alive was experienced as a lack of intimacy in my relationships. It felt like there was a basic dishonesty in my relationships. I felt that we were all engaged in the construction of a mammoth scheme to keep us all distracted. There were many ways I tried to approach this with my friends and lovers, but for many of them, I was too intense, too earnest, and too hard to be around. I felt like a problem and no one wanted to feel the fire of this problem with me. I wanted to be near people who also wanted to explore this possibility and give me insight as to what it might be like on the other side of denial. This brought me to Death Cafés.
>
> *Clare Cross, attendee at the second*
> *Toronto West Death Café in 2015*

The crowd never looks like a crowd that's talking about death. Which is good, because no matter where we hold Death Cafés, we are always sharing the space with others who are enjoying drinks with friends and NOT talking about death. In fact, I often get questions from the regulars at the bar or café inquiring about our party.

> Paul was sitting at the bar with a beer, wearing a baseball hat and chatting with a few other regulars. They clearly knew each other, but not too well. They were talking about the Blue Jays game, with a lot of silence between comments. He overheard some laughter at our tables and asked to join us. I explained that it was a Death Café and we would likely be talking about death. Paul looked at me with the most incredulous expression and mumbled a few words. He noted how intensely everyone was sharing, something so missing from his evening. We were nearly done for the night, so he shared an email address, and came out to the next Death Café, a few months later. He later reported that the Death Café evening had been his best conversation in years, and had made him feel less lonely.

In 2019, I was interviewed by Dr. Gitte Koksvik from the University of Glasgow. She was conducting research on the international spread of Death Cafés.[5] She postulated that the changing demographics of society were demanding both governmental policy responses and also community-level engagement.

> Cultural interventions such as Death Café may be one route to socio-cultural preparedness, affecting the kind of attitudinal and behavioural changes identified by researchers as necessary for building Compassionate Communities.
> *Dr. Gitte Koksvik, Research Associate, University of Glasgow*

✆

Another voice I found speaking about dying and death was Buddhism. I have been a Buddhist practitioner for more than 25 years. It has played a major role in my life for much of this time, and helped me understand the basics of life, and my own purpose on this planet. Buddhism has a lot to say about studying death throughout one's life. In fact, there seems to be plenty about death and the afterlife in most religions, and some might argue that this is one of the prime purposes of an organized religion. However, there seems to be limited interest or conversation about the dying process in most religions. Language reflects values, and it is significant that we have a word in the English language for the pain that comes to loved ones after someone's death – grief – but not really much emphasis on the grief that comes

---

5 Richards, N., Koksvik, G., Gerson, S., & Clark, D. (2020). The Global Spread of Death Café: A Cultural Intervention Relevant to Policy? *Social Policy and Society*, 19(4), 553-572.

leading up to death – only anticipatory grief. There is no special word of its own for grief before death. Buddhism has no special words for grief, but it many words and practices related to the dying process, and even more explanations and practices about the death and rebirth process. Buddhism is universally known for being interested in what continues to evolve after this particular life, and it's not surprising that many Death Cafés include a large number of Buddhist practitioners.

You'll notice that I quote a lot of Buddhism in this book, because there are many practices and principles in Buddhism that deal with dying and death. Buddhism has been an important part of my own exploration about dying and death. You don't need to be a Buddhist yourself, and if you're not interested in Buddhism you can always skip those sections. I find that Buddhism has some excellent maps and language to explain what happens at end of life. It has helped me to make sense of what appears to happen. I hope that by sharing these maps that it also helps you in some way. Or maybe it can help you connect to your own spirituality or whatever you think happens at end of life.

Buddhism has a large group of practices for remembering that death is coming. The impermanence of life is one of the three basic tenets of Buddhism upon which all else is based (the other two are non-permanent self and suffering). For Buddhist practitioners, it is imperative to explore the thoughts, feelings, and sensations that arise as one ponders dying and death, and not only theoretically but one's own death.

For a while I used an App called *We Croak*. It sent messages to my phone five times a day with a quote about death and with a reminder that we will all die. It is based on a Bhutanese practice where one contemplates death five times a day. Some of the quotes were explicitly Buddhist, while others were about death in general. The Bhutanese idea is that by remembering that death happens, it will remind us that life is short and that we can make urgent decisions about living life fully.

> My favourite quote on this App is: We fear pain and its management; we fear the loss of all that is precious to us, including our capacities, our possessions, our relationships, our dignity, and our life; and we fear the unknown – the annihilation of the self.
> *Roshi Joan Halifax, Abbot, Upaya Zen Centre*

To prepare oneself to face dying and death, there are also Buddhist practices of studying the decomposition of the body. These used to be practiced at graveyards, where decomposing bodies could be viewed over time. Practitioners also attended burning pyres, often on the edges of rivers, where bodies were being cremated out in the open. Vajrayana Buddhists also complete visualizations of the dissolution of the body and prepare for the separation of the body from consciousness after death.

Remembering that death is coming to us all is considered to be a useful way to increase the motivation to practice meditation today, and not in the future, when it may be too late. One of the most impactful practices I have taught to my Buddhist Sangha is the Nine-Point Death Meditation. In this practice, there is a rational reminder that death is definite, the time of death is indefinite, and at the time of death, only spiritual practices can help. These reminders apply to all persons around the world, regardless of spiritual belief. The study of dying and death may be avoided by most people, but for the fearless ones willing to contemplate their meaning, the practices are profoundly life changing and life affirming.

❧

And finally, I found the voice of dying and death in the hospice palliative care field. This field brings together the various contributions of hospital, residential hospice, community hospice, volunteers, family members, and spiritual friends, combining them into a holistic approach to dying and death. Hospice palliative care sees the individual as having physical, emotional, practical, and spiritual needs at end of life. A team of professionals and non-professionals works together to address symptoms and needs in the moment, and in a timely and individual manner. Comfort to the dying person is the ultimate goal of care. It is a model worthy of consideration for the entire healthcare field, but for now it seems you have to be dying before you get this awesome and elevated level of care.

Medical help used to focus only on keeping people alive as long as possible. We have made great strides in improving our treatment options, and Canadians are living longer and longer. The discipline of palliative medicine in Canada was defined and started in 1975, and palliative care became a doctor specialty in 1999. Finally, in 2007 it became a subspecialty with standard competencies and training. Since then, the medical field for all professions is scrambling to develop specialized palliative training programs to train the various professionals to help people die better.

In recognition that hospice palliative care requires not only a doctor but also a team to deliver, I noticed that there were indeed various psychosocial and spiritual opportunities for dealing with dying people and their families. Volunteer opportunities with dying people seemed to abound (and have largely replaced volunteering opportunities with seniors), and I volunteered more than 300 hours with dying people and their families in the early part of my career transition. I also highly recommend volunteering in hospice palliative care as one of the most rewarding volunteer opportunities available.

In 2014, psychosocial training for hospice palliative care was still limited, but I gobbled up all I could find. I started with online studies in Thanatology – the study of death – at Conestoga College. I willingly attended the various mandatory and optional volunteer training offerings at the Princess Margaret Cancer Centre and Kensington Hospice. I found a two-year online certification program in hospice palliative care offered by Mohawk College aimed at nurses, and talked my way into it. The Pain and Symptom Management course on medications nearly killed me, with my limited science background and abilities, but I did manage to squeak by and pass, and ended up with a Certification in Hospice Palliative Care.

I moved quickly from being "the student" to being "the facilitator" (and teacher). There were others thirsting for death education, and I soon became an expert. I have led many hospice palliative care education events in the last seven years, and I often include an exercise called "Eight More" (the guidelines for which are included at end of this chapter). It challenges individuals to notice how values change as one progresses through an illness journey towards death. Though it's just a guided imagery exercise, I've never completed it without a significant portion of the group reaching for Kleenexes and wiping tears away. As a simulation, it feels real and brings participants in touch with the reality of their own deaths. It also demonstrates at a visceral level how values change as one gets closer to the end of life.

As I turned 50 and found myself exploring and increasing my own interest in serving others, I found my calling to step into the fire, and to face my own mortality. I leaned into any practice that would help me see that my own life would one day end. I also wanted to share this message with others. The richness that this has brought my life is beyond explanation, and I am forever indebted to everyone who has helped me on this journey and exploration.

I write this book for caregivers to help them learn about the dying process so they may be able to face the dying process fearlessly, helping their friends, family members, and clients who are dying. I want to offer a book that is written not by a doctor, but by a social worker describing the dying and death process and the system that supports it in a language anyone can understand. I want caregivers to clamour to accompany others into the last anthem of life. And I believe that if caregivers are prepared and knowledgeable, they can see when death is 21 days away, and they can make decisions that can reduce the suffering of others. Together we can help more Canadians die with as clear and peaceful a mind as possible all the way to their last breath.

Along the way, you'll read the stories about many dying people and their families that I met on my own journey as both a volunteer and staff professional working in home hospice care, residential hospices, and palliative units in a variety of settings. Their names and specifics have been changed (and sometimes combined) to protect their confidentiality.

Activity 1

Eight More – A Guided Imagery Exercise

Imagine you are going along just living your life. You go to your family doctor for your annual check-up. She runs a few tests and tells you that something has changed in your blood work. She tells you she has found signs of cancer. After a few more tests, she tells you that the cancer appears to be growing slowly. She tells you that her best estimate is that you have 8 more years to live. What goes through your mind? What matters the most to you? What do you do?

You continue to live your life, and generally feel quite well. But after a number of years, you start feeling different. You go back to your doctor. She runs some more tests. And then she tells you that the cancer is advancing. Even with treatment, she thinks you have only 8 more months to live. What goes through your mind? What matters the most to you? What do you do?

By this time, you are no longer working. You spend most of your time at home, but you are happy. You check back with your doctor and she comes to visit you in your home. And then she tells you that there are no more treatment options, and she thinks you have only 8 more weeks to live. What goes through your mind? What matters the most to you? What do you do?

Your health continues to decline as the cancer progresses. You are not able to do much except lie in bed. Your doctor comes to you, and she does not suggest any more tests or treatment. She tells you she thinks you have only 8 more days to live. What goes through your mind? What matters the most to you? What do you do?

You are barely still breathing. Your doctor no longer visits with you, and the nurse assures you that your death will be soon. She tells you she thinks you have only 8 more minutes to live. What goes through your mind? What matters the most to you? What do you do?

You are not really aware of this world, and you are no longer conscious. You hear voices in your room. You imagine that you have only 8 more seconds to live. What goes through your mind? What matters the most to you? What do you do?

1

Introduction to Hospice Palliative Care

The way that Canada does death today is not the way it has always been. Hundreds of years ago, death was real. We cleaned bodies in our kitchens and laid them out for final viewing in our living rooms. We wouldn't have been very old before being asked to care for a dying family member or seeing a dead body up close. Death was normal and it was all around us.

However, medical advances changed all this. We stopped keeping family members at home when they were ill. We sent them to hospitals to be cared for. Since the Civil War in the United States in the 1860s, things changed not just in the United States, but in Canada as well. In Canada, we have started routinely asking businesses (called funeral homes) to take care of our dead bodies. We paid dearly for them to make the dead body look like it was still alive through embalming procedures. Bodies had to be shipped home from the battlefields, and this took time. Embalming allowed people to have a week or more between the death and the burial. Embalming provided enough time for families to meet with funeral homes and make the plan for the funeral, visitation and burial. It allowed people to pretend that they didn't need to think about death until it happened. While embalming has been used in many societies around the world, including use in ancient Egypt, things changed substantially in our era to make embalming become a standard practice for Canadians, regardless of social status.

In the 19th century in Ireland and England, there were residences for dying people called hospices. They provided safe places where the family didn't need to see the dying process. They were often places to be avoided and thought of as only for people who had no one else to care for them.

Despite the increase in hospitalization for treatment in the 20th century, a hospital is often a difficult place for a family to support a loved one when dying. Bells and beepers that are comforting during treatment can be disturbing at end of life. Regular hospital rooms are not made for family members to sleep over, and dying often takes a while. Family members can seem to interrupt the hospital routines of monitoring and treatment, and are not always welcome by staff.

In 1967, Dame Cicely Saunders set up the first place specifically for dying persons. Set up in London, England, she called this place a *hospice*, as in a home for travellers, a place to go "home". Trained as a physician, a nurse, and a social worker, she taught specialized care in a specialized setting for people as they near death. She believed dying people deserved this specialized care.

The term hospice was not the first term used for such specialized death service in Canada. The word hospice in French means a nursing home for poor people and has pejorative connotations, and the suggestion of "a dumping ground of mediocrity of care, signifying the worst of nursing homes".[6] When Dr. Balfour Mount set up a specialized setting for persons nearing death in Montreal in 1974, he called the specialization *palliative care*. (Another setting at St. Boniface General Hospital in Winnipeg officially set up the first Canadian setting a few weeks earlier, but with less publicity.) Dr. Mount based the term palliative care on the Latin term *palliare*, which means *to cloak, to shield, or to protect from the elements*. Dr. Mount published extensively on his new specialization and is credited by most people in Canada for the creation of this specialization here in Canada. Since then, this phrase has spread in use to all corners of the world.

Dr. Balfour Mount is one of the unsung Canadian heroes in the establishment of palliative care in North America. He set up a palliative care unit in the Royal Victoria Hospital (RVH) in Montreal, different from the standalone hospice setting in England. He built on the legacy of Dame Cicely Saunders, and emphasized the medical aid in dying. He was made a Member of the Order of Canada in 1985 for his pioneering work, and later in 2003 this was promoted to an Officer of the Order of Canada, being called the "father of palliative care in Canada" by the federal government.

Dr. Mount considered himself a self-ordained disciple of "Saint Cicely", although he had to earn his way into learning from her by showing up and rolling up his sleeves to do whatever she asked of him at her hospice. He visited St. Christopher's Hospice in London for a week in 1973, and maintained a collegial relationship and friendship with her over the following decades. Given the size of Canada and the fact that roughly 80% of Canadians were dying in hospitals and institutions at that time, he thought Canada could not afford to build standalone hospices like St. Christopher Hospice. A palliative care service at a hospital became the Canadian alternative.

At the time, RVH was known as one of the preeminent teaching hospitals in Canada, filled with visionary healthcare administration. They were willing to take a chance on a new mode of care not being practiced elsewhere. It blended well with the universal health care system in Canada, and the assumption that all Canadians

---

6   Phillips, D. Portraits – Balfour Mount. *Palliative Care McGill.* mcgill.ca/palliativecare

have access to medical care in hospital. It worked well for Dr. Mount, who defined healthcare as "a relational process involving movement toward an experience of integrity and wholeness." He led the way in Canada in recognizing the need for humane and compassionate care at end of life.

The public life of Dr. Mount and his contributions to the hospice palliative care world are better known than his private life. He dealt with testicular cancer at the age of 24, and while it didn't kill him, it taught him much about suffering. He was forced to confront his own mortality at an early age, and was initiated into the club of knowing death up close. Although already a doctor specializing in urology, this experience changed him forever. Years later, in 1973, when his church expressed an interest in hosting Dr. Elizabeth Kübler-Ross who was promoting her book, *On Death and Dying*, Dr. Mount volunteered to organize the event. He gathered a group of doctors to discuss the book and heard Dr. Kübler-Ross describing patients being left to die alone and in pain. She showed them what patients actually wanted at end of life. He was changed forever. He put together a study on what it was like to die at VHC. A few months later, he sought out Dame Cicely Saunders' work in London, and the rest is history.

Only at the end of his own life did he acknowledge how his own cancer journey had primed him to change his specialty to palliative care. Experience with death (one's own or others) at an early age often sharpens the search for meaning, and leads to lives with greater purpose. While it may not be welcome at the time, in hindsight it causes profound pivots in life trajectories.

While Dr. Mount's contribution is significant, he couldn't have made his contribution without Nurse Sue Britton. The voice of palliative care doctors is better documented than other professionals working alongside them, like social workers and nurses. Social workers are generally too modest to think of themselves as expert enough to write books, and it's unknown who the first Canadian palliative care social worker was. What we do know is that Sue Britton, even less known than Dr. Mount, was the first palliative care nurse hired at VHC to work with him. Her self-described mission was "to teach people to not be afraid of dying and that what we have here, life, is just part of the journey, and I would like to teach people how to do it. I can teach people to let go."[7] She began nursing in the 1950s, and was struck by how it was standard to give people the same dose of pain medicine, regardless of who the patient was, their gender, or their pain tolerance, etc. She watched people suffer – one of her greatest lessons. She noted how no attention was given to the family members of dying people, and she found this shocking.

Sue was the lead palliative care nurse on the unit when Robert Buckingham came to her unit as an undercover patient (an assumed name for Robert Simpson), as part of one of the studies that Dr. Mount was funded to conduct. He shared how it felt to have nurses "see" him and offer kindness to him, along with the medical

---

7 Phillips, D. Portraits – Sue Briton. *Palliative Care McGill.* mcgill.ca/palliativecare

care. She claims that this was the real start of palliative care, when professionals learned to treat dying people as if they were people.

On Vancouver Island, in 1978, the Victoria Association of the Dying set up the first visiting hospice service. Unlike the hospital palliative care units, The Victoria Hospice was a grassroots service offered outside of the medical system, and was usually provided in the dying person's home. They provided a volunteer program of support for people in the community who were dying. The hospice provided many non-medical services (spiritual support, companionship, and respite care), and worked closely with the home-based medical services provided by the British Columbia Ministry of Health. They continue to this day to offer community support to dying people and their families, and are the oldest, continuous hospice in Canada.

There has often been some tension between the grassroots programs of community hospices and the hospital-based palliative care. In Ontario, these two arms initially set up separate memberships (The Hospice Association of Ontario founded in 1989 and the Ontario Palliative Care Association founded in 1981) but in 2011, they merged and unified their voice for the benefit of the people of Ontario. The new association was called Hospice Palliative Care Ontario, and a more collaborative approach that combines both together into hospice palliative care was created.

> Everybody wants a better death. We need to change our culture about death. The most important healthcare conversations happen around the kitchen table.
> *Rick Firth, Hospice Palliative Care Ontario, CEO & President*

In 1988, Casey House became the first standalone hospice for people with AIDS in Canada. In fact, it was also the first hospice offering hospice palliative care dedicated solely to people with AIDS in the entire world. It was named after Casey Frayne, the son of June Callwood, one of Toronto's leading activists for social justice, who died at the age of 20 after being hit by an impaired driver. It was originally set up as a hospice, and provided 24/7 residential hospice services for people with AIDS. In 2010, it changed designations from hospice to hospital, as the focus shifted to treating persons with AIDS rather than providing comfort for their final months.

The Dorothy Ley Hospice in Toronto was originally a community hospice delivering medical and psychosocial supports in the home. Dr. Ley was a visionary doctor who believed in the principles of palliative care. At a time when the Canadian medical field was led by men, Dr. Ley forged ahead as a specialist in oncology, working with cancer patients and their families. She had a dream of offering "a more personal and loving alternative to end-of-life care".[8] Dr. Ley pioneered the field of community hospice care in Ontario, and ensured that spiritual care was a primary part of end-of-life care. She believed that the cycle of life, death, and rebirth brings power and

---

8 The Dorothy Ley Hospice. *Who Was Dorothy Ley?* www.dlhospice.org/who-was-dorothy-ley

hope in a time of grief. She chaired the first Board of Directors of the Dorothy Ley Hospice. She died of cancer herself in 1994, but not before she left behind a legacy that promotes "meaning in life and that the spirit does overcome all in the end."

In 2009, the Dorothy Ley Hospice became the first residential hospice in Canada open to all persons dying of any cause. A ten-bed residential hospice was opened in a self-contained building that allowed dying people with a prognosis of less than three months to come to die. They provided 24/7 medical services, in addition to social and spiritual support offered by both professionals and trained volunteers.

In the years since then, many more community and residential hospices have opened in many urban as well as rural communities across Canada. As Dr. Mount predicted, Canada has never had enough hospice palliative services in any location. As the Baby Boomers age and eventually die, the need for hospice palliative care is even greater than before. Canada is training more doctors to specialize in palliative care, building more residential hospices, and training more volunteers in hospice palliative care, and still it's not enough. Surveys show that most Canadians (75%) would prefer to die at home, but the reverse is actually happening. Statistics for deaths in hospital in Canada peaked at 77.3% in 1994, and have slowly been coming down to 61.5% in 2015.[9]

The widespread offering of hospice palliative care is still lagging behind Canadians' wishes. Research shows that more than 85% of Canadians are still dying without any home hospice palliative care.[10] The reason for this is not that they don't want it, but that it's not available. Rural locations and limited community resources challenge the delivery of hospice palliative care, particularly in the northern parts of Canada.

⊚

These three models of care for dying persons have continued to this day throughout Canada – hospital palliative care units, residential hospices, and visiting or community hospices. The term that is generally used to describe the whole of these services in Canada is *hospice palliative care*. (In the United States, England, and Australia, the distinction between hospice and palliative care is more pronounced, and terminology is used slightly differently.) Some communities have greater access to some of these options than others, and access varies greatly between provinces and between urban and rural settings. In some ways, smaller towns have often created the greatest access even more so than large cities like Toronto, Montreal, and Vancouver where there are also more demands for these services.

Hospice palliative care varies by setting, but always adheres to the definition of palliative care put forth by the World Health Organization:

---

9 Arnup, K. (2018). *Family Perspectives: Death and Dying in Canada*. vanierinstitute.ca

10 Ibid.

Palliative care is an approach that improves the quality of life of patients and their families facing the problems associated with life-threatening illness, through the prevention and relief of suffering by means of early identification and impeccable assessment and treatment of pain and other problems, physical, psychosocial and spiritual.[11]

Taking apart this definition, it is clear that palliative care must be offered to not only the dying person, but also to their families, however that is defined. Palliative care is owed to the dying person when they are told that their illness is coming to an end and threatening their life. (The term *life-limiting* has replaced *terminal* as a way of expressing that there are limited treatment options left, but with less implication of necessarily being close to dying.) For many people, there will be treatment options offered into the final days, even if they are dreadful options full of pain and suffering. Dying people are entitled to prevention and relief of suffering from whatever cause. The suffering that is expected is supposed to be identified early, and not just reacted to. And the care must be *impeccable* – not just so-so or good enough. It must be the best we have. It must address all the sources of total pain identified by Dame Cicely. Finally dying people are invited to show up as whole beings with needs related to the whole of our lives. It is with great relief that dying people's spiritual needs can finally be considered, and hopefully met.

There are 5 basic principles that all forms of hospice palliative care must follow:
- Provides relief from pain and other distressing symptoms;
- Intends neither to hasten nor postpone death;
- Integrates the psychological and spiritual aspects of patient care;
- Offers a support system to help patients live as actively as possible until death;
- Offers a support system to help the family cope during the patient's illness and in their own bereavement.[12]

⊗

Medical care often calls itself *patient-centred,* but hospice palliative care truly is. The Ontario Medical Association states that "A patient-centred care system is one where patients can move freely along a care pathway without regard to which physician, other health-care provider, institution or community resource they need at that moment in time. The system is one that considers the individual needs of

---

11 BC Centre for Palliative Care (2019). *BC-CPC: The First Five Years 2013-2018.* bc-cpc.ca

12 Ibid.

patients and treats them with respect and dignity."[13]

It's easier to describe patient-centred care by what it actually looks like. Examples can be found in the flexibility of the rules. For example, if a patient wants food that's not on the menu because they're having nausea, can this be accommodated? Or maybe they miss their pet – can they visit? If a patient wants to get some fresh air – can they go outside? Are buildings designed to make this easier, and are there staff or volunteers around to help push a bed and sit with the patient outside? Is the building designed to make it easy to push the beds outside, as transferring to a wheelchair may not be possible without stressing the dying body? My experience is that these person-centred considerations are much more likely to be given as death approaches than during any other period of health care.

Stories abound of hospice volunteers going the extra mile to make a dying person's favourite final meal, whether it be a Newfoundland Jiggs dinner or a stack of pancakes with real maple syrup. Hospice palliative care rooms are most likely to include access to nature and outdoors in all seasons, and volunteers will gladly help residents spend time there.

Person-centred hospice palliative care is also about letting the dying person make decisions for themselves for as long as possible. Most decisions like stopping eating or increasing or decreasing pain medication can be made by an individual with a low bar of competence. (The decision to request Medical Assistance in Dying requires clear competence, and is an exception, and for good reason.) In this way, many dying people make all their own decisions, and leave almost nothing to be decided by their formal Power of Attorney for personal care. It is not uncommon for people dying of cancer to make all their own decisions of care up to their final weeks of life. This can be a great relief to hear for people who value their independence and dread having someone else take over for them. (Chronic diseases of dementia or stroke may alter this statement, but the dying process itself does not rob one of one's autonomy throughout most of the journey.)

⊚

To paraphrase the old saying, "It takes a village to help a person die well." Death is messy. There are never too many hands, as long as they are busy. Even just sitting together quietly is a very supportive task. There are so many tasks to be done, and people can hopefully find where they are needed most.

Regardless of location, a dying person needs an awesome team around them.

1. **Doctor**: The hospice palliative care team will be directed by a doctor. This doctor may be a specialist treating the disease (like an oncologist treating cancer), or maybe the patient will be lucky enough to have it be their Family Doctor, who

---

13 Ontario Medical Association (2010, June). *Policy Paper: Patient-Centred Care.* content.oma.org

has been serving them for years. The doctor leads the process, but does not often attend much in person.

2. **Nurses**: On the ground, it's the nurses who are in charge. They have even greater autonomy in hospice palliative care and can make more decisions in the moment. (As a result, hospice palliative care nurses are some of the happiest nurses with the greatest job satisfaction. Awesome to have them around you guiding the in-person care team.) Nurses manage the 24/7 care even if family and friends are doing much of the hands-on support.

3. **Personal Support Workers** (PSWs): A dying person needs help with toileting, cleaning, and even moving around. The greatest number of care hours is usually provided by PSWs. It is an intimate job, and it's best if they are well chosen and well appreciated. Unfortunately, their wages are often barely above minimum wage and do not reflect the importance of the role. Also, there is a hierarchy of where they want to work and for whom, so a little kindness to them and a higher-than-usual pay goes a long way to earn their loyalty.

4. **Social Worker/Psychotherapist**: Facing end of life can bring up a multitude of feelings and thoughts, and often it's hard to face these alone. Social workers can speak with both the dying person and their family members, and help facilitate deep conversations before it's too late. They can also help referee conflict that often arises at the end as various people or groups of people struggle for control in a situation laden with meaning and memories. Conflict doesn't go away just because someone's dying, and it may intensify at the end of life. Social workers can also track down resources and referrals, and assist with filling in forms and applying for eligible services.

5. **Chaplain**: The definition of hospice palliative care considers spiritual concerns to be relevant as death approaches, and a multi-faith chaplain can provide support and spiritual guidance. A chaplain can also help facilitate dying rituals and connect with other spiritual leaders, as requested. Patience is a necessary skill of all chaplains, and they often show great patience is sitting with family members through the slow parts of dying. Some chaplains specialize in grief counselling, both the initial grief after the final breath and later after the death as well.

6. **Family members**: Some people die with dozens of family and friends around them. Others choose to go it alone at the end, or with only a few select people. And family may be defined more as select friends than blood relatives. Family members may provide the bulk of physical care, or simply choose to visit and offer emotional support. The number of ways a family shows up at the bedside

of a dying member is as varied as the families themselves.

7. **Volunteers**: Anyone can be a volunteer – both formal and informal. More people volunteer with hospice palliative care than with seniors' programs today, and they achieve great personal satisfaction from it. Volunteers provide administrative support, physical care, vigil support, respite care, legacy work, kitchen help, cleaning, driving to appointments, and virtually any other kind of support. A subset of volunteers comprises those who offer their professional services – music therapy, art therapy, grief support groups, childcare, aesthetician care, pet therapy, Reiki, Therapeutic Touch Therapy, hand massages, and more.

A Non-medicalized Death

If you ask Canadians how they want to die, most will say they hope they die in their sleep. They don't want to see death coming! They want it to be quick and sudden. But fewer than 10% get this.[14] The rest of us will need to learn to see it coming. And if we see it coming, where do we want to die? Again, more than 75% of Canadians would prefer to die at home or in a residential hospice. Although 93% of Canadians live at home at end of life, most won't die there. More than 60% will still die in hospital.[15] And most of us won't see it coming.

There will be a valuable lesson in what impact the Covid-19 pandemic has on future choices and statistics. Researchers generally agree that it is impossible to ensure accurate statistics during a pandemic. A large number of people have died in hospital attached to ventilators trying desperately to stay alive, and this will show up in statistics for this period. Another large group of generally older people died in long-term care homes without ever being transferred to hospital. No one has described a Covid-19 death as a good death, no matter what the location.

Many people continue to work with their medical team on treatment aimed to cure, right up to the very end. This isn't just in Canada, but in other countries around the world as well. I was honoured to be interviewed by Kate Swetenham who visited Canada from Australia on a Churchill Fellowship. She travelled to Ireland, Scotland, England, and Canada in 2018, to meet strategic leaders in both palliative care and end of life care who had developed strategies to guide end of life care policy development. The Australian government was interested to see how other countries have expanded end of life care beyond the boundaries of a health care system. She found a universal medicalization of dying in all these countries, including Canada, which was increasing along with the palliative care specialty.

14 Arnup, K. (2018). *Family Perspectives: Death and Dying in Canada*. vanierinstitute.ca

15 Ibid.

There has been a very real need for palliative care services to return the focus from cure to care at the end of life, and to relieve suffering where possible. Palliative care is now a medical specialty, and with that comes further medicalization of dying. Communities who were once experts in managing end of life are now deskilled. The work occurring in the countries that I visited that have employed the "compassionate communities model" are emphasizing the need for empowering local communities so that they can again be skilled in supporting neighbours and the local community members confidently in all aspects of dying, death, and bereavement.

Kate Swetenham, Nursing Director,
Department of Health and Well-Being

Palliative Performance Scale (PPS)

As mentioned in the introduction, the body breaks down in a predictable way. The tool used by hospice palliative care workers to interpret this is the Palliative Performance Scale (PPS).[16] This tool, created by the Victoria Hospice in British Columbia, has been used internationally to give shorthand to staff and volunteers about the current function of the dying person. Only doctors and nurses are allowed to actually designate the appropriate number, but the system is easy enough for everyone to understand. The PPS dictates what services the dying person needs and is eligible for, as waitlists and some services are determined at least in part by the PPS number.

The PPS is a functional decremental scale, in that it measures how well someone functions in a decreasing way. Fully healthy persons start at 100, the scale goes down by 10s (100, 90, 80...) and at 0 you are dead. The scale is read from top to bottom, and from left to right. If one column happens to drop, the number drops. There are 11 categories, from 11 down to 0.

Three Locations for Hospice Palliative Care

There are three main locations for receiving hospice palliative care. They all provide hospice palliative care, but delivery is different depending on the location. The rules to qualify are different, and the hominess factor can vary significantly as well.

---

16 *The Palliative Performance Scale Version 2* (2001) is reprinted and shared with permission by Victoria Hospice Society. A full image, including notes, is available in the Appendix section of the book.

These 11 categories are organized into 3 stages: **Stable** (100-70), **Transitional** (60-40), **End of Life** (30-0)

There are five observable parameters included in the functional assessment:

1. Degree of ambulation and walking
2. Ability to do activities
3. Ability to do self-care (cleaning and toileting)
4. Intake of eating and drinking
5. Level of consciousness

VICTORIA HOSPICE

Palliative Performance Scale (PPSv2)
Version 2

PPS Level	Ambulation	Activity & Evidence of Disease	Self-Care	Intake	Conscious Level
PPS 100%	Full	Normal activity & work No evidence of disease	Full	Normal	Full
PPS 90%	Full	Normal activity & work Some evidence of disease	Full	Normal	Full
PPS 80%	Full	Normal activity with Effort Some evidence of disease	Full	Normal or reduced	Full
PPS 70%	Reduced	Unable Normal Job/Work Significant disease	Full	Normal or reduced	Full
PPS 60%	Reduced	Unable hobby/house work Significant disease	Occasional assistance necessary	Normal or reduced	Full or Confusion
PPS 50%	Mainly Sit/Lie	Unable to do any work Extensive disease	Considerable assistance required	Normal or reduced	Full or Confusion
PPS 40%	Mainly in Bed	Unable to do most activity Extensive disease	Mainly assistance	Normal or reduced	Full or Drowsy +/- Confusion
PPS 30%	Totally Bed Bound	Unable to do any activity Extensive disease	Total Care	Normal or reduced	Full or Drowsy +/- Confusion
PPS 20%	Totally Bed Bound	Unable to do any activity Extensive disease	Total Care	Minimal to sips	Full or Drowsy +/- Confusion
PPS 10%	Totally Bed Bound	Unable to do any activity Extensive disease	Total Care	Mouth care only	Drowsy or Coma +/- Confusion
PPS 0%	Death	-	-	-	-

1. Hospital Palliative Care Unit

In Canada, hospitals provided the original model for hospice palliative care. Today, nearly every hospital in Canada has a specialized unit for people who are dying. In the larger hospitals, it might be a whole floor or unit. In smaller hospitals, a few rooms might be spread out throughout a hospital. In a hospital setting, it might be harder to know if you're getting palliative care, or just regular care.

However, there are a few signs of hospice palliative care at a hospital:
- Palliative care rooms are single (no doubles or wards);
- Rooms have facilities for family members to sleep over, like beds, benches, or chairs that pull out;
- Meal plans are more flexible with menu items or times available;
- Open visiting hours, or at least extended hours;
- Can handle high care needs with both treatment and palliative care;
- Open to persons with various PPS numbers, and needing hospitalization for stabilization or treatment;
- Prognosis for end of life can be varied, including a long or unpredictable prognosis.

2. Residential Hospice

A residential hospital is a standalone building that was created for the sole purpose of housing people who will be dying soon. Residential hospices provide both medical and non-medical support 24/7 by staff and volunteers. Some residential hospices look like regular houses and are even located in residential settings, while others are more closely affiliated with a hospital or long-term care home and are in the same building or nearby.

For many years, residential hospices were few and far between, and located mostly in large cities. These were slow to take off, but now they are quite popular and there are more being built in most provinces. The Canadian healthcare system is behind the need at this point, and it is scrambling to catch up with the desires of many Canadians. The idea behind the residential hospice is that it is beneficial to have a specialized setting for people who are dying, away from people who are actively getting treatment in a hospital. Residential hospices exist in only Prince Edward Island, Quebec, Ontario, Manitoba, Saskatchewan, Alberta, and British Columbia, and nationally there were only 88 residential hospices in 2018.[17]

Information about future residential hospices is as hard to come by as residential hospice beds themselves, as there is no one place for such information. The situation in Toronto and the surrounding area is representative of the kinds of issues

17 CHCPA (2020). *CHCPA Factsheet.* chpca.ca

in all big cities, not only in Canada but around the world. As of March 2021, there were still only 24 adult beds in Toronto, for a population of 2.9 million people. These are 10 beds at the Kensington Hospice, 10 beds at the Dorothy Ley Hospice, and four beds at the Journey Home Hospice (exclusively for homeless persons). There are 58 more beds promised: Kensington Hospice will get 12 more beds, St. Joseph's Hospital will create a standalone Lake House Palliative Care Centre for 10 beds with a first-ever palliative care emergency service, 10 beds are promised to the Toronto Commandery Hospice, 10 beds are coming for the Neshama Jewish Hospice, Journey Home will create six more spaces for homeless persons to add to their current 4 beds, and 10 beds are expected for a West Park Hospital and Hazel Burns Community Hospice partnership. Many of these hospice plans are announced with great fan fair, but then are hard to substantiate in subsequent years.

Unfortunately, most residential hospices take more than ten years to fundraise the capital needed to build the structure, so delays in opening hospices are notorious. Delays of 5-10 years are considered normal. Many more residential hospices have been announced and promised by the Ontario Ministry of Health. They are spread across the Greater Toronto Area, including Vaughan, Markham, Mississauga, Brampton, as well as Scarborough. Others have also been promised across Canada, and it is becoming common for residential hospices to be linked up with current community hospices to combine services and provide more seamless services.

As a general rule, here is what you can expect at a residential hospice:
- There is no standard number of beds, and they range in size from 3-24 throughout Canada, but 10 is most common number – large enough to support the 24/7 staffing model, but still small enough to be personal;
- All rooms are single;
- Each room has access to a private or semi-private washroom with shower;
- There are facilities for families sleeping over, including limited kitchen access;
- 24/7 healthcare;
- Good for people with or without friends and family visitors;
- No transfusions, IV drips, or most other treatment options, but plenty of other pain and symptom management options;
- Interprofessional support and volunteers;
- Due to need for prognosis of less than three months to live (in most hospices), more beds are filled with people with a cancer diagnosis than any other disease. Other common diseases are advanced heart, respiratory and kidney disease, Alzheimer's, AIDS, ALS and Multiple Sclerosis;
- Most accept patients with PPS numbers 30 and below (a few use 40 or even 50), sometimes higher if the prognosis is for a quick drop or if their pain and symptom management at home was making them at risk of hospitalization.

3. Community (or Visiting) Hospice Care

Community hospice allows people to die at home. It is specifically the most non-medical support for dying, but it is also integrated with medical supports. Services can be tailored to the needs of the dying person and their support team. It is often led by a social worker or counsellor, who provides an assessment and then authorizes other services and referrals. The community hospice support often works closely with in-home medical services, even attending group rounds, where individual patients are discussed and planned for collaboratively.

As a general rule, here is what you can expect with community hospice services:
- Services provided in private homes alongside families and friends;
- Non-medical services offered in conjunction with provincial home health care medical services;
- Offer support and services of longer duration (one year or more);
- Wide range of support services, such as grief support (anticipatory grief and after death grief) by social workers/psychotherapists or chaplains), complementary therapies, volunteer support to patient and family, driving to appointments, and respite care for caregivers;
- Many have bricks and mortar buildings, offering grief support groups for children and adults, art therapy, and treatment spaces;
- Nearly everyone is a volunteer with only a core of paid professional staff as supervisors and fundraisers;
- Patients are accepted much earlier in the diagnosis, with PPSs as high as 50 or even 70, and sometimes with chronic diseases, before they even receive a life-limiting diagnosis.

We like to pretend that Canada is a country with equal opportunity for all, and that all healthcare services, including hospice palliative care, are available equally to all Canadians. As Dr. Katherine Arnup writes in her 2018 research paper, *Family Perspectives: Death and Dying in Canada*, "It is important to recognize that the experience of dying and death, like all experiences in life, from pregnancy and birth onward, are affected by gender, race, class, ethnicity, geography, marginalized status, ability, sexual and gender identity, marital status and First Nation/Indigenous/Inuit/Métis status."[18]

If someone experiences homelessness or lives in substandard housing, it can be hard to access hospice palliative care. Health professionals may not want to enter some homes to deliver home care for fear of contracting infections or bed bugs, or may not feel comfortable delivering services to persons directly on the street. Adapting services can be difficult, and it might bring up logistical challenges or

---

18 Arnup, K. (2018). *Family Perspectives: Death and Dying in Canada.* vanierinstitute.ca

personal issues for the professionals, but it is only fair and equitable to do so. Dr. Naheed Dosani received a Governor General's Award for his work advocating for hospice palliative care for homeless people. He co-founded the Journey Home Hospice in downtown Toronto exclusively for people living and dying on the street. He is the founder and lead physician for the PEACH (Palliative Education And Care for the Homeless) Program at the Inner City Health Associates in downtown Toronto, Canada. PEACH functions as an interdisciplinary mobile street & shelter-based palliative care program and is the world's first model to do so. The team functions through a harm reduction, trauma-informed and human rights approach with one goal in mind: to provide equitable access to palliative care.

I was fortunate to work together with Dr. Dosani on several occasions as he advocated for bringing homeless people into regular residential hospices. He implores us to see how difficult it is to access healthcare equally, depending on where one lives, and makes his contribution by demonstrating the importance of having a supportive physician to open doors. We worked together with other staff and volunteers to ensure that these homeless people felt safe and welcome in the hospices. I confess it was shocking to me that not everyone on the team welcomed them equally, and some, in fact, actively opposed them and considered their needs to be too risky for the others at the hospice. Bias and discrimination certainly followed them into the hospices, and it required conversations and effort to keep the access door open for them.

> When you look at the data, homelessness is a terminal diagnosis of the social determinants of health. The life expectancy for someone living on the street or in substandard housing is between 34-47 years of age. Homelessness leads to poorer life expectancies and more diseases throughout life. Social determinants of health related to housing, income, education, and food security predict quality of life, but also the likelihood of accessing palliative care at end of life. Hospitals tend to focus on the acute issues, and ignore the longer-term issues that might be better treated with good palliative care. We have designed our palliative care services to structurally leave out these people and are collectively responsible for this omission.
>
> *Dr. Naheed Dosani, Lead Palliative Care Physician and Founder,*
> *PEACH (Palliative Education And Care for the Homeless Program,*
> *Inner City Health Associates*

I advocated for dignity for all in my own work as a social worker in home hospice services and residential hospices. I made a point of helping volunteers and staff see the humanity in all people. I applied a social worker's Narrative Therapy approach to my work to tell a life story that doesn't begin with the illness. I welcomed stories about work contributions, love stories at the beginning of the marriage, and travel adventures.

> I'll never forget my work with Manfred. He had been living in a shack without electricity or running water, and was dying of lung cancer. Homecare staff refused to enter to help him. He came to the hospice and fell in love with our unlimited bacon sandwiches. To him, they tasted of love and caring, and he grew to trust us, one bacon sandwich after another. He was understandably suspicious of our caring, and couldn't believe that he deserved the same that everyone else got. He was estranged from his family, and I had to work hard to convince his neighbour whom he had done work for to be his power of attorney, rather than turning to a public guardian who didn't know him at all. He died with a bacon sandwich in his hand and a gentle smile on his face.

Funding Models

It's challenging to talk about hospice palliative care without mentioning the discrepancy in funding models in Canada. Hospital palliative care unit fees are covered 100% by provincial health care making patients feel like the services are "free". Even medications are paid for, which can be expensive at the end of life.

Residential hospices receive partial provincial health care funding to cover professional staff (doctors, nurses, PSWs, sometimes chaplains – not usually for social workers, cooks, cleaners, or management). Funding varies by province, from 30% to 100%, and most residential hospices are not fully funded by provincial health care, but require fundraising as well to meet basic needs.

In Ontario, services in residential hospices are offered free to everyone, but the costs are not fully covered from funding sources. The Ontario Ministry of Health covers approximately 56% of the costs, and the outstanding 44% of costs must be fundraised by the hospice each year. The fundraising portion has to cover costs like heating, food, and all maintenance to the building, as well as the unfunded staff roles. This fundraising requires an effort to the tune of $1-2 Million each year. This operational funding is provided only *after* the hospice fundraises the capital for the building. Because residential hospices rely on steady fundraising efforts, they are often built in affluent communities that do not correspond to the needs of dying people, which leaves many people with fewer resources out.

Capital fundraising must generate in the range of $12 -18 Million, depending on desired size and location of the residential hospice. Imagine trying to raise $18 Million for anything without promising any services in exchange. Understanding the capital fundraising hurdle helps explain why hospices often send out elaborate social media posts when funding is "approved" by the Ministry of Health and capital fundraising can begin, even though it will take years, or even decades, before the capital fundraising is completed, the building built, staff hired, and finally service can be provided to the first dying person.

Community hospices receive tiny amounts of provincial health care funding each year, and fund raise much less. Hazel Burns Hospice is a typical grassroots community hospice in Toronto that provides dying people and their family support from volunteers and case management from professionals. In 2019, they received approximately $250,000 in provincial government funding and provided almost 9000 service hours to 378 clients and their families. This averages out to $661 per client.

Alternatives to hospice palliative care cost more than imaginable. In 2021, one day in an acute care bed costs $1100, while one day in a palliative care hospital bed costs $660-770, all fully funded by the provincial healthcare system. By comparison, home hospice palliative care using community hospice services costs less than $100 per day. It is unconscionable that it takes our Canadian public healthcare systems so long to change over to funding hospice palliative care more fully. Choosing hospice palliative care and ensuring that these services are available to all Canadians doesn't only help people die better, but it also saves money. The goal of palliative care isn't to save money, but it shows that a shift in thinking is needed, and NOW, because it does save money over traditional models of dying in acute care and emergency beds in hospital. In society today, we do not have the luxury of squandering limited healthcare resources.

In addition to provincial healthcare funding, community hospices rely on fundraising events to keep their doors open. They touch an incredible number of lives for an obscenely little amount of money. They are deeply embedded in their communities, and have large numbers of volunteers, many of whom are retired professionals looking for meaning in retirement. Volunteers and staff at community hospices are some of the most compassionate and inspirational people you will ever meet.

Hospice palliative care is constantly changing. In 2020, with the Covid-19 pandemic in full swing, services had to pivot quickly. Community hospice services in particular were hard hit by the pandemic, and volunteers were initially locked out of their service commitments. Eventually the volunteer supports were allowed if they could be delivered virtually, and support to dying persons and their caregivers continued by phone and Zoom video.

> Our first goal, in knowing that the trajectory of the loved one's life cannot be altered, is to make life worth living in the time that we are present. Our second goal is to ease the burden of the family and the caregivers, so that they are strengthened for what lies ahead.
>
> *Jo-Ann Leake, MSW, RSW,*
> *Case Manager at Hazel Burns Hospice*

I have recommended hospital palliative care volunteer opportunities to many, many people looking to engage closely with people, particularly for those interested in exploring their own relationship to dying and death. One of the gems for volunteers is the Healing Beyond the Body (HBB) program at Princess Margaret Cancer Centre. This program has been led by Megan Wexler, a social worker with the University Health Network (UHN), for 6 years already. The services include volunteer psychosocial support to individuals and their families at all stages of the illness journey, not only those receiving palliative care. Topics of conversation can span from family history, current events, the individual's medical journey and even go into fears of end of life and personal anxieties.

I volunteered more than 150 hours with them in my early experience with hospice palliative care, and really enjoyed it. Other volunteers were often young students looking to apply for graduate programs of some kind and wanting some practical experience talking with people, professionals wanting some informal counselling experience, or recent retirees who had worked as professionals and were now wanting to stay busy and had lots to offer. It requires a minimum commitment of one year, but many find the experience so rewarding that they stay much longer, since it is as rewarding for the volunteer as it is for the people "receiving" the services. The volunteers at HBB encourage people to feel empowered in their care and support them in advocating for themselves. They are trained to remind people that they are people outside of the cancer diagnosis, and they provide a space for people to share their personal life stories of living with cancer. Many volunteers also have lived personal experience as a patient with cancer or as a caregiver for a patient that helps them have a deeper understanding and empathy.

Pre-pandemic HBB volunteers would wander throughout the outpatient clinics and inpatient units striking up conversation with those who wanted to talk, and equally as important, never forcing their presence on those who didn't. Throughout the pandemic they began offering virtual connections for people given the restrictions, and they have still been able to support their most vulnerable patients, even if not in person.

I started volunteering in the gastro-intestinal unit, where my role was to casually speak with people in the waiting rooms. This might sound like an odd place to strike up a conversation, but for people receiving cancer treatment, they often drive (or are driven) for up to three hours to get there, and plan to spend the whole day hanging around the hospital getting blood work, chemotherapy or radiation, some scans, and then finally have a meeting with their oncologist. So spending 2-3 hours in a waiting room is just part of it. Being a part of their daylong experience was both a break and an opportunity to check in on feelings, questions, and concerns in a safe way in addition to the formal medical system.

A lot of times family members try to be cheerleaders for their loved ones during treatment but that doesn't always address how the patient is truly feeling, so our volunteers offer a non-judgmental and supportive ear for people to share their inner thoughts and feelings with. We can't change their illness or the trajectory of their disease, but there is immense power and therapeutic release in having a personal connection with someone to share the emotional burden of what they are going through.

Megan Wexler, MSW, RSW, Social Worker and Program Lead
Healing Beyond the Body, Princess Margaret Cancer Centre

Access to Hospice Palliative Care

It might seem like everyone would want to die with hospice palliative care in one of these three locations, rather than in a regular hospital, so why doesn't this happen? The reasons are complex. First, the prognosis of some illnesses is harder to predict than others. Cancer has been measured and researched more often, and some cancers are easier to predict. Diseases, like cancer, that are shorter from diagnosis to death tend to be easier to predict, with fewer variables. It is much harder with chronic illnesses, such as amyotrophic lateral sclerosis (ALS) or dementia, to predict when they will end in death.

Second, there are some treatments that logistically cannot be handled in a residential hospice or a home setting. Blood transfusions, for example, are not usually done in a residential hospice or home, and patients must be ready to stop these treatments before moving into a hospice palliative care setting. Many are not ready until it is too late, and they die in hospital without ever receiving palliative care.

Third, there are limited residential hospice beds. Canada has one of the highest ratios of people to residential hospice beds, so many people die at home or in hospital while waiting for a bed to become available. One cannot always move locations easily at the end, so there is often a tiny window of time for agreeing to move locations, and if the window is missed, it may not be offered again.

And finally, not everyone recognizes the signs in time to make the right decision to transfer to or accept hospice palliative care. Too often, family members will hold out at home hoping for a home death, and then suddenly experience a crisis, call 911, and the dying person gets transferred to hospital. The dying person never stabilizes enough to be moved anywhere else, so they die in hospital, often an emergency department or intensive care unit. Transferring a dying person is a traumatic event, even in a private ambulance, and many people die *en route*, or within a few hours of the trip. It doesn't help that some residential hospices are located in idyllic country settings on bumpy country roads!

❦

Lack of realistic planning often makes dying people try to stay at home as long as possible. But then an emergency happens, and instead of handling it with the home care resources, 911 is called. Did you know that it is against the law for paramedics to not try to resuscitate someone, unless they can find the DNR Confirmation form signed by the doctor in the time that it takes to open their bag? There have been instances of people having DNR tattooed on their chests, but without dates, so paramedics might be unclear if the wishes are current. The first place paramedics look for this DNR form is on the refrigerator. Caregivers need to have *someone* to call in an emergency. There is a human compulsion to call someone, so calling a friend or family member can be useful.

Once 911 is called and paramedics arrive, the dying person is often transported to hospital and taken to the emergency department, and that trajectory can be hard to reverse. In Covid-19 times, this often means the person goes alone to the hospital, and the family or friends may never see them again. Not knowing what happens after you call 911 doesn't make you less likely to experience guilt – it accentuates it and makes it more likely to have regret and guilt.

Many people think they want to have "all codes" forever, which means having efforts made to be resuscitated, regardless of the situation. What they probably don't know is that research conducted in Toronto high-rise buildings reports that the out-of-hospital cardiac arrest survival rate following defibulation and attempted resuscitation varies according to the floor you live on. Survival rate is only 4.2% on the ground floor, 2.6% on the third floor, 0.9% above floor 16, and there were no survivors above the 25th floor.[19] Given that many seniors live in high-rise condos, they might want to consider these statistics as they choose which floor to live on, and as they think about their DNR form. And while this research relates to cardiac arrest, not the planned death generally written about in this book, it shows that people often fail to think out health care decisions, and their full impact.

Dying well requires making the best decision possible at any given moment. Making decisions requires adequate knowledge. You need to know what the options are and how one decision leads you down a path to further decisions. The more you understand the system and the options, the better you can handle the emotions that come up as you make these decisions. Better decisions lead to fewer regrets. Ultimately better decisions lead to greater acceptance of dying and death.

A 2018 study by Health Quality Ontario reports that people are still not getting access to palliative care soon enough.[20] For those living on their own at home, fewer

---

19 Drennan, I.R., Strum, R.P., Byers, A., Buick, J.E., Lin, S., Cheskes, S., Hu, S., and Morrison, L.J. (2016). CMAJ DOI. cmaj.ca

20 Health Quality Ontario (2019). *Palliative Care at End of Life: Report Update 2019.* hqontario.ca

than a quarter of all dying people receive a palliative-specific home care visit before they die. More than 45% start palliative care in their final month of life.

Many of us won't be prepared to see the signs of our loved ones dying, and will delay too long until we don't have any choice but to let them die in an intensive care unit or the emergency department of a hospital, or maybe in an ambulance going to a hospital. Being offered treatment till the end and not seeing death until it is too close to ignore. Away from loved ones. Away from a spiritual practice. Far away from comfort care and a natural way of recognizing death watching it come gently.

But that's not necessary. The final 21 days of many diseases are quite predictable. The sequence of body breakdown is the same, regardless of the disease. The speed may be different, but the order is generally the same. For a small number of dying people, it will be shorter than 21 days, and they will drop quickly within a few days, and often die during the night. For another small number of dying people, their body will continue to breathe for up to 3 weeks (truly!) without any nourishment. My experience is that people who face their dying directly and can speak about it openly tend to move through the final stage more quickly (i.e., less than 21 days), but again, there are exceptions of course, and the exact number of days doesn't mean anything. Nevertheless, death comes all the same. So recognizing the final 21 days is about recognizing death, even if you'll never feel like you ever have enough time.

During the final 21 days, energy lessens and mind and body become focused on only the essential activities for the dying person. The body weakens and then is unable to support walking safely. Then swallowing muscles weaken till eating is not possible, and even drinking water is not an option. Finally, breathing becomes difficult and finally just stops. Let's learn this sequence so we understand the choices and know honestly where the dying person is in the process of dying.

Tibet's famous poet and meditation teacher Milarepa is often quoted saying – "My religion is to live – and die – without regret".

And we can help our loved ones do so, too.

2

Body at End of Life

Consciousness in a human being can be divided into three areas – Body, Speech, and Mind. The dying process likewise impacts these three areas, as the consciousness of one lifetime slowly fades and disappears. This book is broken down into these three categories to further understand the dying process. This process begins at birth for us all, but accelerates quickly as disease progresses. Then, in the final 21 days, there are particular signs that death is approaching in all 3 areas. Recognizing death in the final 21 days requires tracking changes as disease progresses, and noticing the signs as they progress towards the final 21 days. This chapter begins with a look at what happens at the body level.

There are many ways to really understand death, but the most obvious way is through the senses and what one can see in the body. Teaching children about death involves reflecting on what the body is doing. Children get this at a very basic level. They watch animals die and see how the body stops working. When we don't dump *our* fears on kids, they remain interested in that line between life and death. They have a natural curiosity about this line that socialization removes from us.

As mentioned in the introduction, the body breaks down in a predictable way. The tool used by hospice palliative care workers to interpret this is the Palliative Performance Scale (PPS). Hospice teams frequently start shifts with staff and volunteers sharing the PPS of all patients. This gives a shorthand communication of what might be expected for that patient. Numbers can remain stable for days or weeks, and then change quickly. Numbers generally go down, but can occasionally go up when things like medication or location changes happen. Shifts in numbers might also occur in response to people coming in and out of the dying person's life, like final visits from a child or close friend. While it's not good to rely too heavily on numbers, and it's important to always see the person in front of you as the in-the-moment expert of what they need, PPS numbers can be helpful to give a summary of what is happening at the body level.

PPS numbers are used to determine what services are appropriate. This brings up the question of when to start palliative care. For the higher numbers (100-70), patients might get mostly treatment, and need little symptom management. However, many treatments used today for a variety of diseases are quite aggressive and destructive to the body. Chemotherapy is one example of a treatment that produces a lot of side effects, in addition to treatment effects. As a result, patients may need palliative care symptom management to be able to tolerate treatment, and non-curative treatment and palliative care to treat symptoms may go well together.

Illness Trajectories

It is possible to imagine what the final stages of dying might look like after a patient receives a life-limiting illness diagnosis. There are four basic illness trajectories, and most diseases will fit closely with one of these. These have various times associated with them, and they reflect general patterns.

Doctors have learned much about the typical trajectories of particular diseases, and this can be useful when a doctor is asked to give a prognosis to help make decisions about an individual's future. These trajectories depend on so many variables that they really must be seen as general patterns and not specific prognoses. Individuals have so many variables relating to prognosis that it's important not to be

Trajectories of Dying

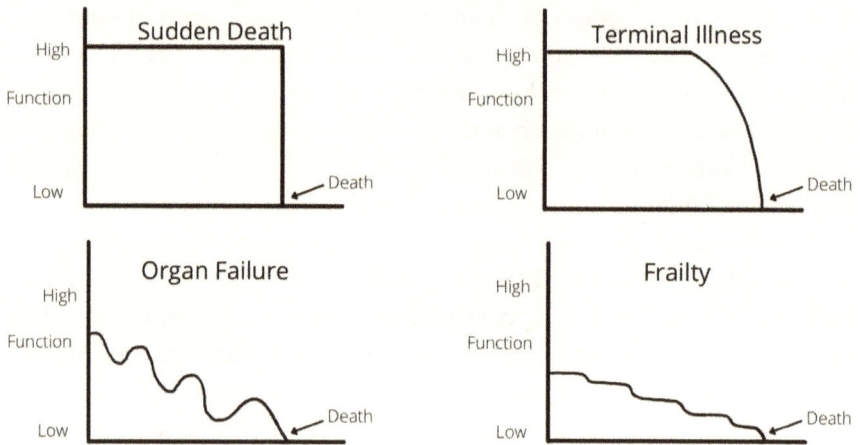

simplistic about predictions.

1. **Sudden Death**: Healthy living and then a sudden drop to dead in less than 24 hours. A heart attack is a common example of sudden death. My friend's mother was living on her own. She was seemingly healthy and independent. My friend spoke with his mother one day and she seemed fine. A week later he got a call from the local police saying she had had a massive heart attack. Her friend had called the police when she didn't answer her phone and they broke the door down to find her dead. Many people think this is the best trajectory, but it is terribly hard on the people remaining to have no advance warning.

2. **Terminal Illness**: This pattern starts with a period of healthy living, and then "shortly" after a diagnosis, maybe one week to ten years, death comes with a sharp decline in health that never gets better than before the diagnosis. This is the trajectory of most cancers. Some cancers are faster and more aggressive, while others are slower, but the pattern is the same. For some cancers, there is a double cycle, in that the cancer is treated successfully the first time, and the patient returns to normal (or nearly normal) life functioning for a period of time, and then the cycle repeats, and this time ends in death.

3. **Organ Failure**: The organ failure pattern appears with heart, lungs, kidneys, and other necessary organs wearing out. There are typically many crises, with each one seeming to be the last one. But then the person stabilizes, gets a wee bit better but never as good as before the last crisis, and carries on. It's unpredictable and tiring for loved ones to wonder each time if it's the last one, and one often doesn't know until the end. This trajectory is common with chronic obstructive pulmonary disease (COPD – the umbrella term for emphysema, chronic bronchitis, and asthma).

4. **Frailty**: Frailty is inevitable as chronic diseases add up and we live longer. The chance of being diagnosed with cancer for the first time peaks for people in their 60s and then drops off after this. [21] People over the age of 70 are much more likely to slowly decline in health, with one or more chronic illnesses, like diabetes, dementia, or congestive heart failure (CHF), as well as a host of other lesser chronic diseases, that cumulatively weaken a body and ultimately bring death. When one says a person dies of "old age", it is often one of these frailty situations that brings on death, sometimes finished off by pneumonia, considering that old age itself is not a disease.

PPS numbers can be laid upon these illness trajectories to begin to understand what the disease journey might look like. For example, when a person gets a cancer diagnosis, they may find they can live their life with a PPS number fluctuating between 70 and 100 for months, years or even decades. However, at a certain point, there will be a change in function that drops their PPS number down. This is evidence that the cancer is probably growing. Different cancers have vastly different growth speeds, so time might vary, but the trajectory is the same. Understanding the trajectory will make it easier to make the decisions related to informing others to visit, when to take time off work and start the caregiver benefit, and even when to plan for the 24/7 vigil.

Dying people need guides, and this is why the time to get referred to a palliative care team is much earlier than previously thought. It is easier to notice the

---

21 Government of Canada (2019). *Fact Sheet Cancer Canada*. canada.ca

PPS fluctuation with a knowledgeable guide. Caregivers who have never witnessed death before or read anything about the dying process should not have to be the guide for their loved ones. This book is written to help prepare caregivers, and provide them with a death education that is not otherwise available.

When palliative care was first offered, it was identified as a discrete phase in the illness journey *after* the treatment phase, and *just before* death. Later, recognition was given to offering it earlier, even at diagnosis of a potentially life-limiting illness and slowly increasing the palliative care as the treatment decreased. A final model supported today, but not often enough put into practice, is the overlapping model of sometimes more treatment and sometimes more palliative care as the disease goes up and down in severity. It is challenging to figure out how to move beyond creating the model to actually operationalizing it during a period of competing needs for healthcare resources.

A doctor once told me that at the point of diagnosis, doctors often try to make a referral for palliative care and the patient and family don't want to hear anything of it. The doctors feel bad because they believe it would be helpful for symptom management. But once the journey moves along and death seems imminent, the patient and family request palliative care and the doctors hesitate because they believe that the next treatment may be just what the patient needs to recover. It's seemingly hard to get everyone on the same page for hospice palliative care at the same time!

Hospice palliative care can be useful to address a wide range of pain management and symptom relief. As the body is breaking down and heading towards death, there are many different ways for the body to react. Health care professionals must have flexibility and expertise to figure out what would make the dying person feel better.

The 2017 Framework on Palliative Care in Canada identified four priority areas:
1. Palliative care education and training for health care providers and caregivers;
2. Measures to support palliative care providers;
3. Research and the collection of data on palliative care; and
4. Measures to facilitate equitable access to palliative care across Canada, with a closer look at underserved populations.[22]

Hospice palliative care aims to reduce suffering and improve the quality of life for people who are living with life-limiting illnesses through the provision of:
1. Pain and symptom management;
2. Psychological, social, emotional, spiritual, and practical support; and
3. Support for caregivers during the illness and after the death of the person they are caring for.[23]

---

22 Health Canada (2018). *Framework on Palliative Care in Canada.* champlainpalliative.ca

23 Ibid.

Palliative Care Models

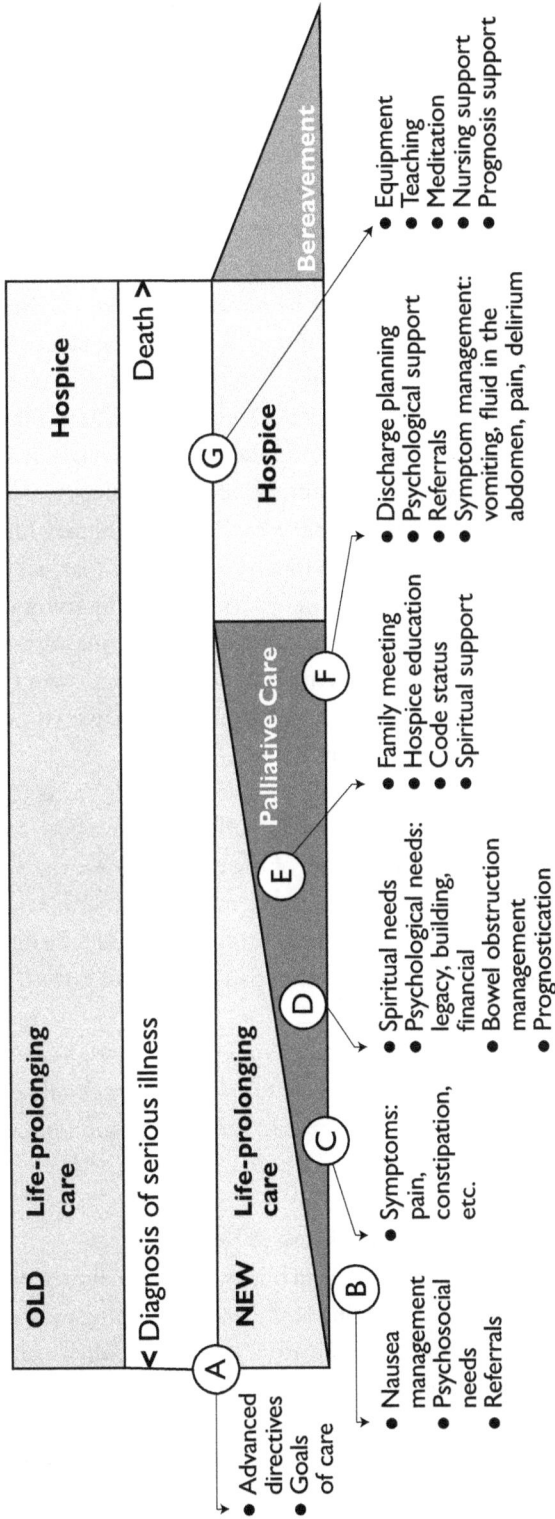

OLD	Life-prolonging care	Hospice

< Diagnosis of serious illness

Death >

NEW Life-prolonging care

Palliative Care

Hospice

Bereavement

(A)
- Advanced directives
- Goals of care

(B)
- Nausea management
- Psychosocial needs
- Referrals

(C)
- Symptoms: pain, constipation, etc.

(D)
- Spiritual needs
- Psychological needs: legacy, building, financial
- Bowel obstruction management
- Prognostication

(E)
- Family meeting
- Hospice education
- Code status
- Spiritual support

(F)
- Discharge planning
- Psychological support
- Referrals
- Symptom management: vomiting, fluid in the abdomen, pain, delirium

(G)
- Equipment
- Teaching
- Meditation
- Nursing support
- Prognosis support

In looking at pain, there are two aspects to consider – the physical sensation of pain and the reaction to the sensation. The reaction, or the suffering, is based on our personal, cultural, and spiritual view of pain and whether suffering is good. If someone has had a past experience of pain that was ignored or minimized by their caregiver, they will be more resistant to noticing the pain when it returns, and thus their personal experience increases their suffering.

There are different cultural views of pain and whether it is better to express it or better to deny it. There is a cultural view believed by some people that people who get cancer bring it on themselves by not expressing themselves sufficiently in their lifetime. This unfair condemnation can be devastating to a person with cancer who feels judged for the diagnosis. Some cultures encourage expressing pain and feelings with loud sounds, while other cultures support stoicism and the suppression of feelings. All of these cultural views impact the way that pain is experienced and expressed.

Gender also plays a role in cultural views and influences the relationship of the dying person to pain and how they handle it. Males may find themselves downplaying their pain, and trying to tough it out rather than acknowledging the pain and seeking help for it. Females may react to pain by using it to ask for support, and thereby noticing even slight changes in pain. Or maybe these roles are reversed when combined by family patterns and the response to pain follows opposite conditioning. Regardless of gender conditioning to pain, pain is a subjective experience influenced by minds, as much as bodies.

I wish I could say that we all use our spirituality to better manage pain, but sometimes religious views increase the suffering. I have been told that it is accepted in some traditional religious views of the body to blame the person for causing the disease. As if the body is expected to live forever, and the breakdown is a sign of disbelief in God. Understanding what meaning pain has for a dying person is helpful in understanding what a statement of pain means and how to best treat the pain.

The cause of pain can be located in a variety of regions of the body:
- Arthritis – low back pain, painful joints (hips shoulders, knees, hands);
- Musculoskeletal – compression fractures of spine and ribs;
- Neurological – irritation or compression of peripheral nerves and/or spinal cord;
- Diabetes – lack of circulation to hands and feet;
- Cancer – deep sensations in bones, intracranial pressure in head;
- Cardio-vascular – angina of the heart, cramping pains;
- Gastro-intestinal – constipation and nausea, often exacerbated by the use of opioid medications.

Palliative care embraces many non-medicinal ways of relieving pain. Volunteers and family members are encouraged to learn these methods, and in particular to learn what their loved one prefers when they experience pain. Dying is personal, so it's helpful to really listen for what it's like and to be as helpful as possible to the person in front of you.

Nausea: Serve favourite foods, in small portions. Ensure a comfortable environment. Provide companionship during a meal. Don't nag and force someone to eat for your sake.

Weakness: Plan activities around their most energetic time of day. Move around and exercise when tolerated. Schedule naps.

Thirst: Provide mouth care frequently. Encourage small sips of fluid. Be creative with favourite drink sips (latte coffee, mouthwash, scotch!). Provide ice chips to suck on, even when they are no longer drinking. Moisturize lips with a lip balm.

Fever: Apply cold compresses. Keep room well ventilated. Take off some layers. Offer cool drinks. Get outside for fresh air if it's still possible.

Jaundice (yellow skin from liver failure): Get into the sunshine, even briefly. Provide good skin care, washing, and moisturizing, as often skin gets very itchy.

Hiccups: Elevate the person's head with pillows to decrease exertion used to breathe. Place a blanket roll between the mattress and springs. Request a hospital bed that can be raised easily.

Vomiting: Clean up the vomit without complaining. Offer mouth care. Ventilate and deodorize the room so everything smells clean again. Provide a cloth for the head.

Constipation: Increase fluid intake. Add roughage to diet, if it can be tolerated. Encourage exercise and movement, even mild exercise. Offer prune juice diluted with warm water. Give plenty of time and space to have a bowel movement in privacy.

Insomnia: Plan relaxing nighttime activities, such as reading (or being read to), or watching a calm TV show. Prepare a quiet, dark room. Offer a warm blanket straight out of the dryer.

Mood changes (crying, increased confusion, irritability): Talk about what it's like to have pain all the time. Normalize all feelings and thoughts. Don't pathologize talking about being depressed or afraid, and watch for moods to go up and down.

Skin Irritation/Pressure Sores: Keep skin clean and dry with daily washing. Move positions regularly. Hold uncomfortable positions for a limited time only (10 minutes) and remember to change back without delay. Ensure proper body alignment in bed or chair. Apply gentle massage with oil or lotion to areas of pressure over the bony prominences. Order a hospital bed that moves up and down. Switch to an air mattress that puffs air in different places to simulate movement.

Did you know that the best way to prevent pressure sores is good hygiene? Regular washing of skin removes dead cells. Bed baths with a washcloth and bowl of warm water work well to clean skin and often take much less energy than showering. Providing a sponge bath is not only practical, but it's also deeply nurturing and soothing, and anyone can learn how to do it safely. The beautiful bath at the residential hospice is the least used room of all.

Everyone's greatest fear at end of life is dealing with pain. There are two distinct kinds of pain. One kind of pain is acute pain, which has a beginning and an end. It diminishes as the cause is treated and healed. Words that describe acute pain are sharp, dull, aching, and burning. While it is intense, one knows when it started and one knows it's going to get better. The person suffering from acute pain tends to be willing to accept treatment to alleviate the discomfort knowing that the condition will be short-lived. Outside of dying pain, acute pain is also experienced after dental surgeries, childbirth, broken bones, and burns. Most acute pain can be easily treated with medications, and the person returns to previous functioning. Acute pain at end of life often signifies a change in the disease, and every effort should be made to address it immediately, non-medically as well as medically.

The other kind of pain is chronic pain. Chronic pain can last for several months, even years. It continues, though the cause is healed. It becomes more difficult to describe the quality or location of the pain. The individual suffering from chronic pain may also suffer from depression, anxiety, and fear of exacerbating the condition. Personal reactions to the suffering are more pronounced for chronic pain, as extenuating circumstances become much more significant to predicting the outcome.

Some common causes of pain are arthritis, cancer, neurogenic pain caused by nerve damage, psychogenic pain having no known cause (which occurs more often than imagined, despite how much Western medicine has advanced), and head or back injury. Many of these chronic pain issues are then exacerbated by life-limiting diseases and acute pain.

Pain affects a person in different ways:
- Physically – unable to get comfortable, reduced movement, decrease in energy;
- Emotionally – increased irritability, depression, anger, worry, and a lack of appreciation for positive emotions also happening;
- Intellectually – unable to focus or concentrate, brain fog, inability to do simple math, distracted mind;
- Socially – lack of interest in others, inward focus, decreased tolerance of groups;
- Spiritually – both increased or decreased interest in spirituality, depending on meaning assigned to pain.

At end of life, it is common to be unable to use words to express pain. There are other ways of noticing if pain is present. Some common ways to determine if pain is present is by noticing grimacing, moaning, excessive sleeping, tenseness of body, elevated respiration, and a general uncooperativeness. If these responses occur during a specific action, such as attempting to move positions, it is likely that pain is present, even if the dying person is not expressing this in words.

Pain Scale

A key principle in palliative care is to constantly monitor and assess a patient's comfort level. The Edmonton Symptom Assessment System (ESAS) [24] is the most common measurement of pain used in Canada. It can be used early in the diagnosis phase, and also throughout the journey. When I volunteered at the Princess Margaret Cancer Centre, I witnessed that every patient was asked to complete an ESAS questionnaire before every visit with their doctor. I encouraged patients to think of this as a communication tool to share what symptoms had changed since their last visit and identify symptoms that were most distressing to them currently.

Each ESAS is entered into a program that identifies trends and compares numbers with previous numbers. Tracking symptoms allows for immediate changes, but also signifies to a doctor when diseases are changing, and helps a doctor communicate back to a patient what might be happening next.

The ESAS was originally developed by the Regional Palliative Care Program, Capital Health, Edmonton, Alberta in 1991. It is an integral part of a comprehensive assessment strategy. It monitors the intensity of symptoms in nine areas. It is self-administered by the patient to express the intensity of symptoms. Staff and family members can assist with it, if necessary, but it is ideal to hear directly from the patient.

Scoring the ESAS is extremely simple. Scores of 0-1 mean literally no pain. Scores of 2-3 mean the pain has no effect on activity and is usually unobservable and not often mentioned unless asked. Scores of 4-5 mean the pain is moderate and uncomfortable, and affects movement. Although the patient may be up and about, the pain is often observable and usually mentioned. With scores of 6-7 the pain is moderately severe, and the patient is generally distressed, and has significantly decreased mobility. The pain is always observable in some way, and the patient frequently talks of pain and requests relief. With scores of 8-9, the pain is severe and horrible. Often the patient either lies very still or is very restless, and is demanding of relief from the pain. At scores of 10, the pain is extreme. It is excruciating, there is extreme agitation, and the patient is screaming for relief. More than anything, it is important to notice when there are changes, and to make sure the team of helpers is aware of these changes.

---

24 Watanabe SM, Nekolaichuk C, Beaumont C, Johnson L, Myers J, Strasser F. A multicentre comparison of two numerical versions of the Edmonton Symptom Assessment System in palliative care patients J Pain Symptom Manage 2011; 41:456-468. 2. Bruera E, Kuehn N, Miller MJ, Selmser P, Macmillan K. The Edmonton Symptom Assessment System (ESAS): a simple method for the assessment of palliative care patients. *J Palliat Care* 1991; 7:6-9.

Alberta Health Services

Affix patient label within this box

Edmonton Symptom Assessment System Revised (ESAS-r)

Please circle the number that best describes how you feel NOW:

No Pain	0 1 2 3 4 5 6 7 8 9 10	Worst Possible Pain
No Tiredness *(Tiredness = lack of energy)*	0 1 2 3 4 5 6 7 8 9 10	Worst Possible Tiredness
No Drowsiness *(Drowsiness = feeling sleepy)*	0 1 2 3 4 5 6 7 8 9 10	Worst Possible Drowsiness
No Nausea	0 1 2 3 4 5 6 7 8 9 10	Worst Possible Nausea
No Lack of Appetite	0 1 2 3 4 5 6 7 8 9 10	Worst Possible Lack of Appetitie
No Shortness of Breath	0 1 2 3 4 5 6 7 8 9 10	Worst Possible Shortness of Breath
No Depression *(Depression = feeling sad)*	0 1 2 3 4 5 6 7 8 9 10	Worst Possible Depression
No Anxiety *(Anxiety = feeling nervous)*	0 1 2 3 4 5 6 7 8 9 10	Worst Possible Anxiety
Best Wellbeing *(Wellbeing = how you feel overall)*	0 1 2 3 4 5 6 7 8 9 10	Worst Possible Wellbeing
No _____ Other Problem *(For example constipation)*	0 1 2 3 4 5 6 7 8 9 10	Worst Possible

Patient Name _____

Date *(yyyy-Mon-dd)*

Time *(hh:mm)*

Completed by *(Check one)*
☐ Patient
☐ Family Caregiver
☐ Health Care Professional Caregiver
☐ Caregiver-assisted

Body Diagram on Reverse

07903(Rev2015-08)

Side A

Signs that might indicate pain in children are:

- General body tension – clenched hands, fist, hunched shoulders, protective posturing, guarding;
- Tense facial expression – unable to smile, whimpering, twitches;
- Constant fidgeting – moving around with restlessness might indicate a full bladder, boredom;
- Nervous habits – biting lip or nails, hair twirling, repeating actions;
- Unexplained withdrawal – inability to be interested in others;
- Change of general tone of voice – strained or high-pitched tone of voice.

Please mark on these pictures where it is that you hurt:

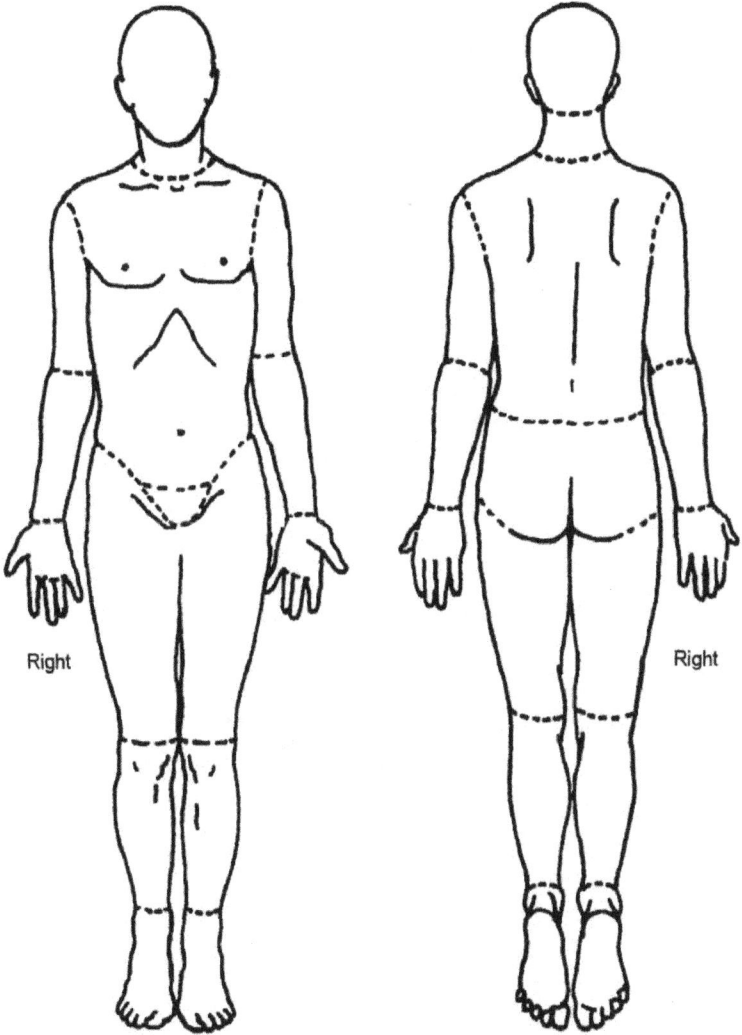

Right   Right

It may be harder to judge pain in children or people with developmental delays who are dying (remember: *everyone dies*), so a faces-based pain scale can also be used.

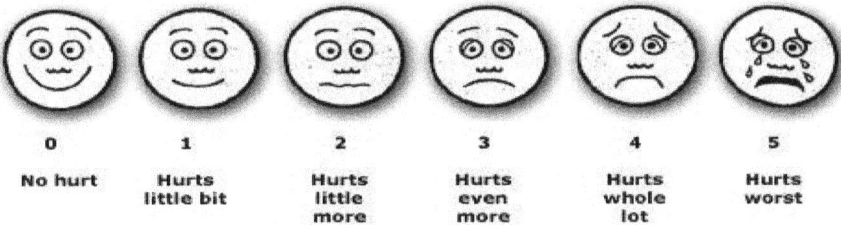

0	1	2	3	4	5
No hurt	Hurts little bit	Hurts little more	Hurts even more	Hurts whole lot	Hurts worst

Standard Orders

One of the most important things to understand about nurses being in charge of day-to-day hospice palliative care relates to the concept of Standard Orders. Essentially, upon admission or beginning homecare, the patient switching to palliative care is encouraged to stop all their life sustaining medications. Examples of the life sustaining medications include statins for high blood pressure or insulin for diabetes. The palliative care doctor replaces the old life sustaining medications with symptom-related medications. They pre-authorize a list of medications for the patient that may be used to treat the most common complaints and symptoms at end of life. The list of likely complaints includes pain, nausea, shortness of breath, constipation, anxiety, insomnia, and noisy breathing (death rattle).

The orders are standard, in that all admissions receive some collection of authorizations personalized to their situation. Opioid pain medication is the only medication that must be authorized by the doctor (the Most Responsible Physician, or MRP) each time there is a change. Otherwise, if a patient can't sleep and it's 2 am, a nurse can administer the medication prescribed for insomnia without checking with the MRP first. Fast service. Fast reduction of suffering. Satisfied dying person.

It takes a special kind of nurse to work in hospice palliative care. Those that choose this speciality are some of the most caring and empathetic people I have ever met. Nancy Hall is one of these originals who joined the movement back in its infancy in Canada. Like so many professionals (and volunteers) working with dying people, she considers it her calling.

> I didn't choose a specialty in hospice nursing to be my career. I believe it chose me. When VON Peel initiated its first Hospice Palliative Care team in the '80s I joined for a new experience, the challenge of what was seen as a tough job, a bit prestigious perhaps if you could stick with it. Only over time did I recognize how comfortable and at home I felt sharing this experience with individuals and their families. It was the first time I felt truly engaged in nursing where it touched people (myself included) at every aspect of our being – physical, emotional, mental, and spiritual. There was never a need to look for new experiences, challenges, or satisfaction beyond what was happening every day.
>
> *Nancy Hall, RN, BScN*

For caregivers, it is important to find your team, and then remember that you are on this team. No one should ever try to make decisions totally on their own. Palliative care is based on constant monitoring and responding.

A simple way to identify the monitoring steps in this care model is ORRD:
- Observe – changes in the individual
- Respond – remember what your scope and responsibility is and then respond accordingly
- Report – to your supervisor/medical team/family members
- Document – your observations

There are so many non-medical care responses to try to reduce pain before turning to medications, particularly if it is important for the dying person to have a clear mind at end of life and be able to communicate with you. The setting has a lot to do with the sensations that arise for the dying person. As much as possible, create a comfortable environment with no conflict between people. Play music, whatever the dying person likes, whether classical, spiritual, or rock and roll. Arrange for a comfortable airflow with fresh breezes. Bring in suitable lighting that is not too bright or fluorescent. Ensure that there are familiar objects in the room, like photos or paintings – objects that remind the dying person of their life and the things that matter to them.

Time moves very slowly in the final weeks. One primary task of loved ones and visitors is to help pass time. Provide distraction from waiting for death. Consider reading aloud (books, magazines, or newspapers), especially if the dying person's eyesight or concentration levels have been compromised. Hold conversations and tell stories, reflecting back over the dying person's entire life. Bring supplies for creative activities, like scrapbooking, painting, or other legacy projects. Get outside and take short strolls or just sit outside in the sunshine (weather permitting, of course).

Regular touching activities (like hugs and kisses) are often reduced as the body no longer looks or feels like it used to. Senses are often heightened as death approaches. Providing a warm or cool face cloth can be much appreciated. Offering to wash hair, or even just brushing hair, becomes an act of love and caring. It may not be possible to have full aesthetic care, but attending to nail care or a facial shave often makes the dying person feel more normal, if just for a moment. Applying lotion or massage oil (almond oil is a good choice) to hands or feet doesn't require a massage therapy degree, as long as it's gentle and supplies used are made for sensitive skin.

> My friend visited her 72-year-old father who was dying of prostate cancer at home. He was still responsive and able to speak, and was enjoying visits by his adult children. One day, my 45-year-old friend visited and decided to climb into the hospital bed with him. They giggled and told stories of times long ago. She felt like a child again and was able to remember the good times they had had together. Although they had often been stiff and reserved as adults, she appreciated one final gift of going back to her childhood. He died the next day, but she treasures this memory forever.

One of the things that happens to the body as it breaks down is that it becomes hypersensitive. The negative aspect of this is that diseases which might otherwise be fought off can no longer be fought off. Infections must be managed carefully to ensure that nothing new comes to the dying person that reduces their quality of life. The most common infections that threaten dying people are the kind of infections that threaten most patients in hospitals – Pneumonia, Streptococcus, and most recently COVID-19. Even something as simple as a urinary tract infection can be the final cause of death, although only to someone who is near the end already from either a chronic or acute disease. These infections are all transferred through droplets and if infections are onsite, a dying person must be carefully protected by caregivers wearing Personal Protective Equipment (PPE), like masks, gowns, and gloves.

Fighting off infections is extremely important when trying to get more years out of life. However, at end of life, succumbing to infection is not necessarily so bad. An infection, like a "nice pneumonia", can be a faster and easier way to go. Many people write into their Advanced Care Plans (ACPs) to deliberately choose to NOT take antibiotics to fight off infections when they are receiving palliative care already. It might be better to go from a quick infection than a long chronic disease.

When AIDS was first identified, there was fear of contracting HIV through caregiving. It has since been learned that it is only spread through needle sharing, blood transfusions, and sexual activities that exchange bodily fluids. Today, protecting patients who are HIV positive is understood to be as easy as applying universal precautions and good hygiene involving proper hand washing and equipment sterilization. Fortunately, today, people who are HIV positive are welcome in residential hospices and receive community hospice services, and their status is no longer required to be noted or shared. There may still be some fear and stigma found in volunteers regarding contracting HIV, and therefore AIDS, but there need not be any special consideration given beyond these universal infection precautions.

The Ending of Eating as Death Approaches

Death is not caught from a dying person – any more than a dying person can share death. But caregivers sometimes cause an early death by not understanding the role of eating as death approaches. Families often believe that they can stave off death by keeping a patient eating. This is one of the biggest myths of all time.

The easiest, most fearless task one can accomplish over the age of 50 is to weigh oneself weekly. The purpose is not to worry about whether you've put on a few pounds or not, but to monitor your health and see if you have lost weight. When a person loses more than 10% body weight in a month without trying, it's time to visit a doctor and get checked out. Some disease is usually at work and beginning to show its impact. Even for non-cancerous illnesses, weight loss is often the first indication that something is wrong.

Eating is an imperative in all cultures, and there are elaborate rituals surrounding the sharing of food. We imagine that if a person doesn't eat much for a day or two, they are starving. We watch them lose weight and tell ourselves that if they just ate a few more bites of food, that they will gain weight and be healthy again. We truly believe that it's possible to buy more time by forcing or cajoling the dying person into eating. We forget that what goes in, must come out. If the kidneys are failing and the bowel is blocked, the pain of keeping the excess in the body is harder and not worth the effort. For some reason, it is harder for the family to recognize when the dying person doesn't want to keep eating than it is for the person who is dying. The dying person commonly recognizes how dying feels in their body and accepts the changes more easily than family members.

Let the dying person decide what to eat and how much! Allow for tiny portions of food, even if an effort was made to prepare that food. Don't make the dying person feel bad for eating only a little. Make whatever the dying person thinks they want, even if it's different from what they used to love. There's no need to point out that their opinions are different now, and don't argue about who knows best. Expect tastes to change. Hormones are changing drastically at this time, and simple foods are generally preferred. Keep eating as a social event if the dying person has energy for this, and invite the dying person to sit at the family table at dinner, even if they themselves are no longer eating.

Empathy is based on one person relating to how someone else feels, and therefore being able to respond appropriately to the hurting person. Unfortunately, most caregivers have no idea what it's like to die, and have no experience with the body shutting down and no longer being hungry or thirsty. Be wary of false empathy at end of life, when you think you know what the dying person needs, based on your own experience in your own life. The place this shows up most often at end of life is when dying people no longer want to eat or drink. To a caregiver applying empathy from their own life, this means the dying person must be starving and dying of thirst. This is what I call "false empathy", and is not grounded in the experience of dying people.

Don't let yourself imagine that a dying person who has stopped eating and drinking is starving or thirsty. The dying person may exist for days living on a few bites of food while still having great conversations and being fully engaged in connecting with loved ones. Their mouths may be dry and need mouth care, but their bodies may not be thirsty. At a certain stage in the disease journey, dying people are not like healthy people who would feel hungry and thirsty when not eating or drinking for days. A dying person's body is shutting down and is living life in slow motion, and no longer has access to those same eating experiences. Be prepared to listen to the dying person's wishes and notice when they are ready to stop eating and drinking.

Everyone will stop eating and drinking at some point before death. It is one of the more significant signs of the final 21 days, and it naturally occurs in everyone. However, the Voluntary Stopping of Eating and Drinking (VSED) is a choice – a decision – one that more and more people are learning that they have the right to choose. It is not suicide. It is not euthanasia. It is more like a fast. It is just a decision. A rational choice at the right time. And it requires the right place.

Voluntary Stopping Eating and Drinking is the bravest decision a human organism can make. It can challenge the human imperative that wants to stay alive by recognizing that moment when quality of life is no longer worth fighting for. It is effective when this lifetime is meant to be over soon. If one attempts VSED too early, nothing happens. Life continues just as it is.

However, if VSED is chosen at the right moment, the body listens to the decision and death happens swiftly. The total stoppage of food and drink triggers the kidneys to fully shut down. It's like the body has been given permission to let go into death. Hormones are released that create joy and bliss, and it is easy to feel at peace. There is often an ease and even light-headedness that is described as pleasant. Pain is often described as decreasing, and breathing is more relaxed. This euphoria may be the physiological result of the analgesic effect of not only the fast, but more directly from the dehydration, assuming drinking water has also totally ceased.[25] Dehydration causes drowsiness, but encourages a pleasant, relaxed mind. This is a lovely state of mind for end of life.

The final stages of end of life happen more quickly after the final food and drink are consumed. Combined with the right mind state (described later in this book), VSED prepares consciousness for a quick departure and a clear mind at the moment of death. People report less pain and symptoms following the decision to stop eating and drinking, as if the pain receptors are turned down as the mind and body together accept death.

> I met a man in his 50s who came to the residential hospice with a PPS of 40, yet told by his oncologist that he was in the end stages of pancreatic cancer. He reported that he had fought other cancers, and now that he had a 4th cancer diagnosis, he was "done" with life. He refused all treatment for this final cancer. I accompanied him to the dining room in his wheelchair on his admission date. He asked to speak with a doctor about his prognosis. His doctor considered his presentation and admission notes and reported a prognosis of five to six weeks. The patient was furious and stated that he wished no more food or water and foretold that he wished to be dead in three days. And he was. He got exactly what he requested.

---

25 Compassion & Choices. compassionandchoices.org

VSED is a somewhat controversial decision in the medical world. Nurses in Ontario are forbidden by the Ontario Nursing Association to suggest it to patients. Patients at long-term care homes will be fed (including being force fed), even if they verbally and with full competence request to stop eating and drinking. There is a fear of legal action by families if the long-term care home withholds food and drink under any circumstances. Patients living anywhere other than their own homes might not be allowed to request stopping eating and drinking until swallowing is no longer possible. Patients may have difficulties convincing family members that they are still competent if they decide to do this sooner than the family is ready to hear.

It is important to know the law if you are thinking about VSED, as it is considered suicide in some parts of the United States and other places around the world. In those places, activating VSED may make an insurance policy null and void. VSED should always be the choice of the dying person, and fear of being a burden to their loved ones is not a good reason to allow it prematurely.

However, there comes a time when nurses will determine that the dying person must stop eating. This is not considered VSED. This determination to stop feeding the dying person is made when the swallowing muscle is no longer able to move the food around the mouth and down into the esophagus toward the stomach. The clearest sign that this time has come is when a dying person starts to "pocket" food, that is, the food that is put into the mouth just stays in the mouth sitting in pockets in the cheeks, not able to be swallowed down. Nurses remove this food with their fingers and either suggest switching to liquid diets or encourage stopping feeding completely.

Dying people who are fed after the pocketing time are actually putting their lives at risk. Food that is not properly swallowed is at risk of slipping down into the lungs rather than stomach, which leads to aspiration pneumonia. Aspiration pneumonia interrupts the 21-day progression and may shock the family by what seems to be a premature death, if only by a few weeks.

There are different religious and spiritual views regarding VSED. Buddhism emphasizes impermanence, and this principle has strongly impacted my own way of seeing death. I see impermanence everywhere around me and in every moment. Buddhism clarifies this principle so beautifully in describing how the arising and passing away is the essence of life. Some Buddhists and people who place great emphasis on the awareness of breath generally support the role of VSED and the fearless choice to say goodbye to this lifetime. More traditional Theravada Buddhists may not support VSED because they see it as a form of glorifying death, as the Buddha condemned, but most Mahayana Buddhists support the practice. VSED increases the chance of a clear mind at end of life by allowing the natural shutting down procedure of the body to do its thing. VSED is not at odds with hospice palliative care principles and can be practiced at most residential hospices, as well as personal home settings. Discussing this eventual decision with family members in advance is crucial in reducing conflict at end of life and addressing concerns of any family members in advance will help ensure that this request is not unsupported when the time comes.

One does not need to identify as a Buddhist to see the benefit of speeding up the final days and weeks of life. Memories and quality of life are not limited to the final weeks. Life is for living fully, and when the end is near, it is time to accept it. Using VSED to reduce the suffering at the end of life is a worthwhile intervention, and one we should all be better acquainted with. Readers may be better acquainted with Medical Assistance in Dying (MAiD), which is the Canadian form of assisted suicide. This intervention will be addressed later in the Mind section of the book.

Watching the decline in PPS numbers helps someone to know when the right time to initiate VSED has come. Diseases vary, trajectories vary, timelines vary, and yet the march to death follows a decidedly common path for the body. The first thing to notice is a marked weight loss. Weight loss without trying is an indication of disease or illness. Many people spend so much of their lives trying to lose weight and know the effort involved. So, when the body decides to lose weight without trying, this is a bad sign.

We are used to thinking that empathy is useful when we are caregiving. In many ways it is, but when it comes to decisions around stopping eating, it is no longer helpful. If we are using empathy in the usual way, we imagine the dying person is starving. Or maybe thirsty. We imagine they want to keep living like this. The best use of real empathy is to imagine ourselves in exactly their shoes. In case you are asked to make decisions on behalf of the dying person at this stage, it maybe be helpful to ask yourself whether you would want to keep living like this? Would you actually want to keep eating and trying to extend this miserable life one extra day, or even a week? A body that is shutting down does not feel hunger like a healthy person. We need to separate ourselves from the dying person and truly see them as they are and believe them when they tell us that they do not want to eat or drink any more. This is one of the hardest things to do, but it is also one of the greatest gifts of love to do well.

Losing weight triggers an overall energy drop and triggers a drop in PPS numbers by reducing overall functioning. Major weight loss might indicate the cachexia stage of cancer when the body can lose up to 50% of its normal weight in a matter of months as the disease moves into its quick growing stage. Hospital beds are designed to be able to weigh someone in it without having to leave the bed. Nurses sometimes weigh patients to determine how fast cancer is growing by the speed of weight loss. Weight may go up again closer to end of life, not from increase muscle mass and health, but from edema, which is swelling caused by fluid trapped in the body.

PPS numbers of 40-100 can go up and down for months or even years depending on treatment decisions and the disease itself. During this time, it can seem like the disease is disappearing, and indeed it does often rest or go into remission. However, there is a moment of no return to health, and the rest of the journey is toward death, and this moment can be difficult to notice in time. This is the crossing over between living and dying, when there is no more to be done to stop the dying process.

Body at 21 Days

All diseases impact the body and its ability to support movement. The ability to walk to the washroom is crucial for many people to retain a certain level of independence. Some dying people choose to wear briefs or have a catheter inserted for urine throughout the day to conserve strength and energy, but make the daily walk to the washroom for the bowel movement. At some point, a nurse (or sometimes occupational therapist) will determine that the dying person can no longer do so. If the dying person is still at home, this is often determined by a fall when trying to walk.

Many people consider the end of walking to be a determining factor in deciding whether to extend the life or not. Walking is not itself the factor, but the independence factor of managing one's own toileting is often considered a "dignity" issue.

Once the legs can no longer support the body, this is evidence of the beginning of kidney failure. This is the right time to initiate stopping eating and drinking, if you intend to do this intentionally. The PPS is dropping from 40 to 30. From here, the 21-day count begins. For most people the final 21 days will be spent totally in bed. Food will be very limited or not at all. And then drink too becomes limited, and mouth care for dry mouth is the primary preoccupation. Of course, there is lots of variability in the exact number of days for each of these stages, and it is possible to be eating and drinking on the day one dies. And for others, the lack of food and water might take more than three weeks to reach an end. But the sequence is consistent.

Some people have very simple body needs in the final 21 days. They need no food or water, and are simply taking sips of air. Pain pumps are already hooked up and pain is being managed, and there are few changes. In fact, if anything, pain seems to decrease, as they get closer to death.

Others are not as fortunate. Sometimes the body does surprising things, and crises happen daily. Sometimes bleeding or vomiting is extreme. Or pain spikes unpredictably and no matter what nurses do to treat it, the pain persists. Orifices can spurt colourful substances, bodies can go septic and toxic overnight, and people can experience delirium and confusion that makes them try to get out of bed and run away, even if they haven't walked in weeks.

When the body can no longer walk (PPS drop to 30) is generally a good time to enter a residential hospice, if that is the plan. It is extremely comforting to have medical support 24/7 just to answer questions in the middle of the night. It can also allow the caregiver to take a break and prepare for the last breath, and not feel totally burnt-out and almost miss it. Also, it can be good to have the many volunteers around for distraction and support if time starts to slow down.

If dying at home is the plan, the final 21 days is when the primary caregiver will want to be available fulltime and not distracted with work or other caregiving needs (like children). There should always be a backup plan, just in case the final 21 days are really hard and it becomes impossible to stay at home, without serious problems for the caregiver. If dying at home becomes too challenging, it can be helpful to consider whether a residential hospice or inpatient hospital palliative care unit might be better than an emergency department admission.

Regardless of your decisions as your loved one comes to the end of their life, 21 days will never seem like it is long enough to be with them. Be prepared for your mind to trick you into believing that you will still have more time, or that maybe the dying person will experience a miracle and get better again. When PPS drops to 30, that's it. It's too late for physiotherapy. It's too late for a new treatment. The time has come to accept that death is coming soon.

3

Speech at End of Life

Speech is the words between caregivers and a dying person as death approaches. It includes grand speeches, formal conversations, and lots of whispered words. For some dying persons, much is made of final expressions of love. For others, more is thought about what has been said earlier in life, and end of life is relatively quiet. But for all, speech is the communication between the dying person and their family members, friends, and the courageous ones who accompany them on the final journey.

There are many types of families, and all seem to show up at end of life. Family, in the broadest of definitions, is the people you love and the people who love you back, the people you feel safe around, and the people you can count on to be there when you need them. It is not defined by biology, marriage, or even by home. Family is complicated and messy, and even more so at end of life! In my experience, it is not uncommon for ex-partners to come back into the picture, for long lost family members to show up, and for friends to really step up and show who matters. I've learned never to make assumptions about who is in the room (or bed) and I always try to be welcoming to anyone brave enough to show up for the dying person.

There are so many kinds of families. One defining difference in families is how they express conflict. Some are open communicators, passive-aggressive, completely in denial, or good problem solvers. Affection is expressed so differently – either loving and close, completely closed off, or with anxiety. The feelings that are safe to express can range from love, anger, guilt, sadness, and hope.

> Families are diverse, and so are family experiences of death and dying. Many things can affect how people experience end of life within families – it is a complex interplay of choice, culture, and circumstance. Many families don't discuss death or dying, grief or loss. Research shows not discussing these fundamental aspects of life can impact the well-being of dying people and their families when tough conversations need be had, plans need to put into place, and important decisions need to be made.
>
> *Nora Spinks, CEO of the Vanier Institute of the Family*

The roles that family members play range from primary caregiver, spouse, sibling, power of attorney, friend, peacekeeper, cook, cleaner, to chauffeur. At end of life, there are never too many people! We are finally recognizing that these roles all need support and there are a growing number of caregiver support groups that ensure that the caregivers' needs are met. It is so easy for caregivers to be stretched and stressed, and not to notice and take care of their own needs.

Caregiver is often the best generic job title to describe the hard role of death assistant. Some people resonate with this title more than others, as some people find that it's too formal and sounds more like a paid professional. Others prefer the terms *carer* or *loved one*. Regardless of what you call yourself, if you have responsibility for the health and wellbeing of a person who is dying, you are a kind of caregiver.

The attitude of the caregiver towards the person who is dying and the words and tone they use is critical to how the dying person experiences the dying process. Communication is hard under regular life circumstances, but doubly so at end of life. One of the most important goals of hospice palliative care is to provide care with dignity and respect to the dying person. But maintaining this dignity is challenging when "something happens – a fall, a new symptom, a bad medical report – and you find yourself frantically trying to adjust to the 'new normal.'"[26] Caregiving may be one of the most destabilizing and difficult roles in a whole lifetime, so make sure you don't judge yourself too harshly for less than stellar performance over years or even decades.

> It's important to give the person you care for as much dignity
> and respect as you can. They're looking for a little control over their
> lives as they lose a lot of it. It's the little things that count.
>
> *Dr. Katherine Arnup, academic,*
> *family caregiver, life coach, and author*

Conversations with dying people are not completely different from regular conversations. However, the pace at end of life can feel much different, and usually slower. There may be more time between questions and answers. Conversations might be shorter to conserve energy of the dying person. Conversations might move easily between profound pondering about the great beyond to talking about bowel movements. Conversations might focus on the dying person, or the dying person might play more of a listening role and let their families carry more of the active conversation, depending on where they are in the process.

Katherine makes a number of suggestions in her book on caregiving that easily apply to a variety of situations:

---

26 Arnup, K. (2015) *I don't have time for this!: A Compassionate Guide to Caring for Your Parents and Yourself.*

- Don't assume you know everything;
- Ask open-ended questions and wait for a response;
- Demonstrate patience and forbearance, more than you ever thought necessary;
- Find compassion for self and others;
- Accept that the situation is as it is; and
- Imagine walking in others' shoes.[27]

Conversations about the 'elephant in the room'

It is so common for families to just not want to see what's happening. For caregivers to ignore the signs. Conversations about dying are often the last thing loved ones want to bring up. As such, too often conversations about the obvious become 'the elephant' in the room. It takes a certain flair to bring up these conversations for the first time. Often, we think of these awkward conversations of being something we can do one time, and that we'll do down the road.

Kathy Kortes-Miller believes that conversations about dying and death are an integral part of life that deserves and demands acknowledgement and respect. She also brings a lighter tone and humour to these conversations, utilizing her social work training, as well as her own personal experience with cancer. In her book, *Talking About Death Won't Kill You: The essential guide to end-of-life conversations*, she reminds us that challenges learned earlier in life can also be applied to end-of-life decisions. She encourages us to look death in the eye and face the challenges collectively. One conversation at a time.

> Death is not a medical event. It is a social process. Yes, it's difficult. Yes, it's sad. But that's part of the cost we pay for loving someone, for having the privilege of getting to know them, and caring for them, and growing old with them, whatever that might look like.
> *Kathy Kortes-Miller, PhD, MSW, Assistant Professor,*
> *School of Social Work, Lakehead University*

Psychosocial Needs by PPS

Caregivers are expected to engage in many conversations with dying people. For some caregivers, these conversations come naturally, and you may have plenty of life experience to help you figure out what to say. But often, you might need a bit of help having these conversations, and you would benefit from meeting with a hospice palliative care social worker or psychotherapist who specialize in these conversations. In some hospice palliative care settings, these psychosocial conversations

---

27 Ibid.

Needs by PPS

ADMISSION →

→ DEATH

↑ How are you today? ↓ ←

30 ... 30

Orientation to hospice

Person outside disease

Medical journey

Spiritual beliefs

Cultural needs

Family system + history

Family conflict

Psychosocial aspects of care + EOL

Medicating for comfort

Toileting

Stages of dying

Reduced intake

Cognitive changes

End of talking

Preparing for next stage

EOL signs + symptoms

20 20

Care for the caregivers

Grief + bereavement planning

Supportive friends + family

How to communicate with friends + family

How to involve children

Friends + visitors

Locating + arranging resources

Funeral/ Memorial Service planning

Paperwork, referrals, support

Financial considerations

Wishing for the end

MAiD interest

Discussing the final end

10 10

How to support the dying

Focus on the day-to-day

Holding space

Meaning-making

Encourage storytelling

Who should be there at the end?

Death awareness or denial

Regrets

EOL unexplained phenomena

0 0

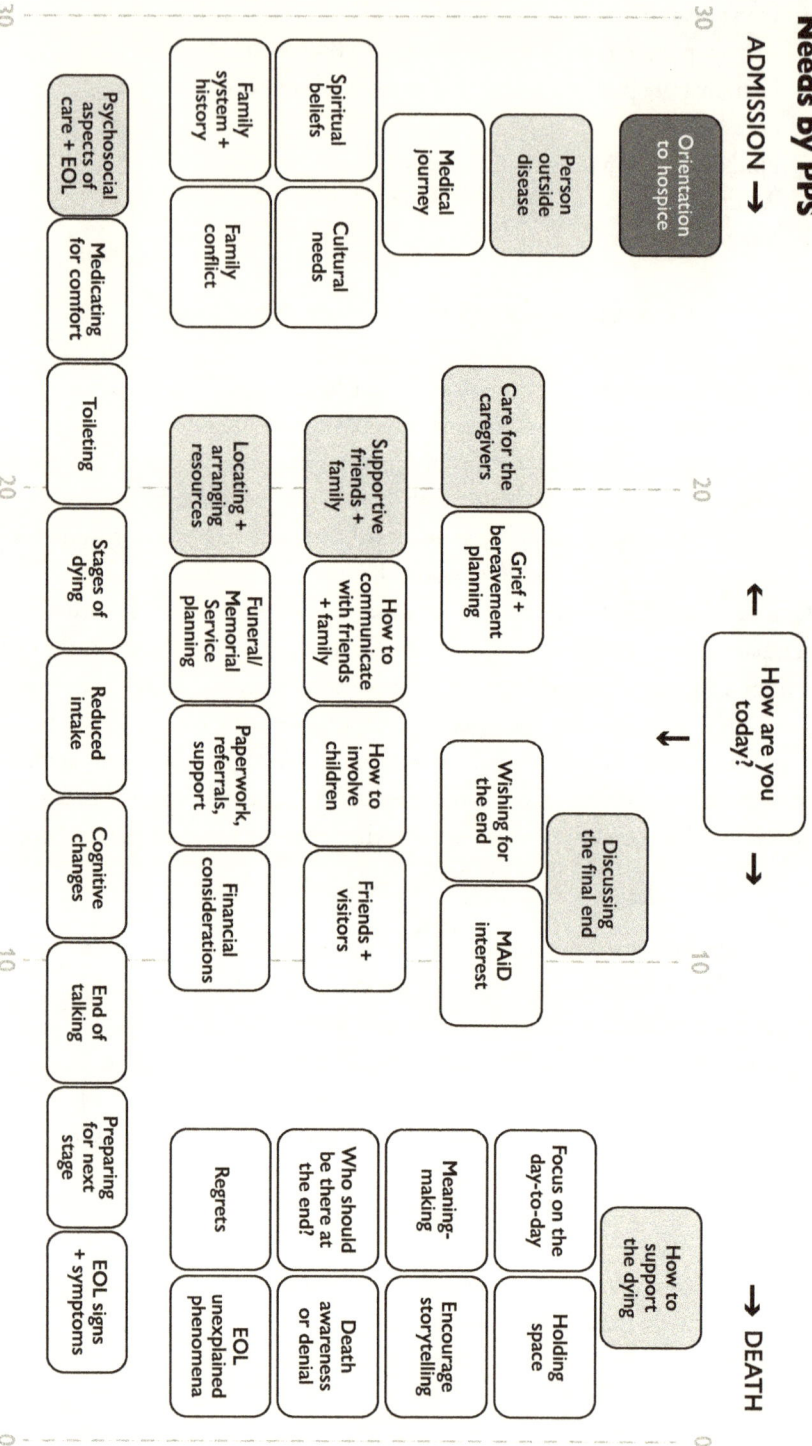

Shared with permission from Bethell Hospice and Carolyn Gibson Smith.

Themes of Needs by PPS

30 Orienting toward the resident and his/her supportive friends and family. Identifying caregiver support needs, family systems issues, administrative requirements.

20 Doubling down on caregiver support, while coming to terms with impending death. Helping the caregiver understand palliative care, EOL processes, and support the resident.

10 Support to be fully present in the room, understanding what's happening, holding space for the dying, making meaning of life while caring for those who continue living.

Text shared with permission from Bethell Hospice and Carolyn Gibson Smith.

are also offered by trained volunteers in the role of "Resident and Family Support."

Several years ago, when I was working as a hospice palliative social worker at Bethell Hospice, a residential hospice north of Brampton, I was lucky to work with a bright and analytical social work student by the name of Carolyn Gibson Smith.[28] What started as a conversation about hospice social worker competencies on our commute to the residence turned into a qualitative research study. At her urging, we conducted this study on the kinds of psychosocial conversations that dying people and their family members find helpful. We were looking at conversations that paid staff have, rather than the one kinds of conversations that unpaid caregivers might have. Carolyn analyzed our clinical notes using a grounded theory model of research to determine whether psychosocial needs changed by PPS. We presented these findings at several hospice palliative care conferences around the Greater Toronto Area in 2018.

As social work was still relatively new to Bethell Hospice, and research and training opportunities were limited around what might constitute hospice palliative social work practice in Ontario, we wanted to take our cues from patients and families as to how we could best serve their needs. In reviewing options for research in the sensitive environment of a hospice, grounded theory research seemed like the least-intrusive option.

The best thing about grounded theory research is you start with the data and see if it leads to a theory, rather than starting with a theory and testing it. In pouring over pages and pages of transcripts of psychosocial conversations with hospice clients and their families, we were able to first identify peoples' concerns by conversational content, then by themes. Ultimately, we could say with confidence that,

---

28 Smith, C.G. carolyngibsonsmith.com

at Bethell Hospice, within our social work program, there were specific themes we could identify at each descending level of PPS. These themes could help us quickly orient, for the kind of support that might be required on any given day, as we crossed the threshold into a client's room.

We realized that conversations at PPS of 30 were radically different from conversations at PPS of 10. Early conversations at higher numbers focused more on getting to know the person outside of the disease and direct conversations about dying. Later conversations were more often with family members, and were more focused on self-care for the caregiver and signs of end of life for the dying person. Overall, we identified about 40 different conversations that hospice social workers needed to be comfortable with in order to assist dying persons and their families.

We noticed that we needed to become comfortable bearing witness to secrets that dying people wanted to unburden themselves of at end of life. We learned about siblings and children that were never spoken about before. We learned about mistakes made that had not been admitted to previously. We navigated between current families and secret trysts who all wanted a place around the bed of the dying person. And most of all, we tried to make room for as many family members as the dying person wanted to spend time with, even if they didn't all get along. We made schedules and helped create space to have estranged family members see their loved one a final time. We moved between the legal roles of power of attorney and the family roles of people who just wanted information and didn't want to be left out. More than anything, we helped families focus on the needs of the dying person and ensure as calm and quiet a setting for them as possible.

The compass heading for a PPS score of 30 thus became "Reorientation: concerns of living while dying." We could expect clients and their families to be making sense of their medical journey, needing to share the stories of medical hopes and regrets. They'd be wanting to understand the processes, terminologies and competencies of hospice care, and coming to terms with the new logistics of a foreseeable death, including pragmatics such as paperwork. These conversations were still very much about the concerns of the living, dying person, and it was critical for all hospice workers to be focused on getting to know the patient's stories, preferences and priorities.

Sometime after the flurry of adjustment to hospice, PPS would drop to 20. "Recognition: concerns of dying" would become our compass heading. Questions about signs and symptoms of the dying body, what visiting family and friends might expect emotionally, and how to manage connections with friends and family were important – but at this point they'd be coming more from family and friends than the dying person. We'd also see the beginning of active reminiscence and storytelling, which seemed to provide comfort to the dying person and those in the room.

Finally, with a PPS of 10, we'd be ready to pivot toward "Remembering: living in an altered world." At this stage, we'd be supporting friends and family to contin-

THEORY
From living to dying to living on...

30 REORIENTATION
Concerns of living

A strong focus on the dying person as a person, their loves and people; making sense of the health journey, the systems and paperwork.

10 REMEMBERING
Living in an altered world

Preparing to continue on without the loved one. Requires meaning, stories, supportive family and friends. Preparation for bereavement.

Resident, caregiver/s, and friends + family are central

20 RECOGNITION
Concerns of dying

Understanding the signs of dying, the emotions that arise, re/membering, re/connecting with friends and family.

Text shared with permission from Bethell Hospice and Carolyn Gibson Smith.

ue on without the loved one, having prepared them for what to expect in this stage. Meaning-making, story-telling and holding space would be paramount. When done well, this stage seemed like good preparation for the not-dissimilar work of actual bereavement, which would likely begin within days.

The shorthand for the stages revealed by grounded theory became, 'From living (PPS 30), to dying (PPS 20), to preparing to live on in an altered world (PPS 10)'.

Carolyn Gibson Smith, MSW RSW,
Social Worker and Researcher

We also learned that social workers needed to be comfortable bringing up conversations that dying people and family members were often embarrassed to speak about. It is common at end of life for dying people to experience paranormal experiences of strange time and space continuum that have them seeing people who have died, knowing things that people have not said out loud, or remembering stories that had previously been forgotten that now wanted to be told.

While this research has not yet been published, replicated, or peer reviewed, it has greatly impacted the way I provide psychotherapy and support to dying people and their friends and family in my private practice. There are so many conversations to be had between dying people and family members. Conversations that should have been had years ago, but people always think there's more time. As often as not, these conversations do not happen unless someone new (like a social worker or other end of life volunteer or staff) is in the room.

Healing Family Relationships

I have a favourite palliative care doctor, Dr. Ira Byock, who wrote a seminal book about end-of-life conversations back in 1997 called *Dying Well.*[29] He revolutionized palliative care conversations by describing how conversations between family members reduced end of life pain more than pain medication. As a doctor, he spent more time calling up estranged family members than he did trying to offer treatment to dying patients. (He later combined the first two parts about forgiveness below into one part, and refers to them in this way in his latest book, *4 Things That Matter Most.*)

He summarizes these family conversations as having five primary themes. Not all families need all five themes addressed, and often these thoughts are never spoken aloud, except at end of life. This is the only time a family can bear such intimacy.

1. Please forgive me.
2. I forgive you.
3. Thank you.
4. I love you.
5. Goodbye.

A woman in her 60s arrived at the hospice with a PPS of 30, and stayed there for a couple of weeks. She had a doting husband and daughter who both visited often. I noticed that there wasn't much talking in the room often, and everyone seemed really happy when a volunteer or staff entered, as everyone would perk up more. When her PPS dropped to 20, I leaned into the conversation by asking her if she had said everything she wanted to say to her family. She surprised me by saying that her family had never really articulated things much, but she wanted to learn to try. So the three of us, including her husband, met that afternoon and I invited her to say any of the five final things that Dr. Ira Byock suggests. She nailed all of the four things she spoke about, and he answered them back to her. They both had tears streaming down their faces. When they

---

29 Byock, I. (1997). *Dying Well: Peace and Possibilities at the End of Life.*

finished, she asked me if I could set up a similar meeting for her and her daughter. We did that meeting the next afternoon, and again, she was able to articulate all five wishes to her daughter and they were both ecstatic. At the end of that meeting she turned to me and told me how she wished she could have met me and done this 20 years before. Before she had to know she was dying.

We all have unfinished business. It's common to think that there will be more time in the future to resolve things with loved ones. Then one day, more time doesn't come. We need to embrace the impermanence to allow ourselves to feel the motivation to get on with it!

Dignity Therapy

There are many ways to organize conversations at end of life. Another method is based on the Dignity Therapy work by Dr. Harvey Max Chochinov in Winnipeg, Manitoba. The goal of Dignity Therapy is to bolster the dignity of the dying person and reduce their suffering and the feeling that they have been reduced to just their disease. In his book, *Dignity Therapy: Final Words for Final Days*,[30] he describes both helpful perspectives and practices.

Dignity Preserving Perspectives:
1. Continuity of self
2. Role preservation
3. Generativity/legacy
4. Maintenance of pride
5. Hopefulness
6. Autonomy/control
7. Acceptance
8. Resilience/fighting spirit

Dignity Preserving Practices:
1. Living in the moment
2. Maintaining normalcy
3. Seeking spiritual comfort

Practically speaking, this modality invites the dying person to think about what their values are and what matters most to them. With the help of a therapist or trained volunteer, they create a narrative document to share with professionals treating the dying person to ensure they see the person and not just the disease. The process strives

---

30 Chockinov, H.M. (2011). *Dignity Therapy: Final Words for Final Days.*

to help professionals, as well as all caregivers, understand all the thoughts, feelings, and sensations that arise when caring for the dying person, and to remember the dying person had a whole life and not just a final chapter of dying. It is a formal therapy that requires months of work and culminates in a sharable document, and a guide for caregivers to see the entirety of the person outside of their illness.

Death is really challenging for those who are deeply attached to loved ones. It is common to imagine that if your loved one died, you couldn't go on. Buddhism teaches love and compassion for all through Loving Kindness Meditations, and is known for its imperative of non-attachment, even to family members. Not that one isn't allowed to love one's family, but rather that love and attachment is not limited to family, and in fact everyone in the world is loved *as if they were your own mother... or family member*.

Legacy Work

There are many ways to remember a person. To focus on their impact on the world is to keep their memories alive. People fearlessly facing their own deaths will often want to engage in legacy projects for their loved one and friends. These tasks cannot be done in the final 21 days, and are rarely completed at a residential hospice. The focus in the final 21 days is on moving on. Even if the dying person is still responsive and communicative, the volition or interest in completing a legacy project will be gone. Opportunities for legacy work must be done well in advance of moving into hospice care, ideally at diagnosis or when the focus is still on this earth.

Here are a number of suggestions for meaningful legacy projects that dying people might want help completing in the final six months leading up to death.
1. Writing or making video memoirs
2. Writing letters to be given to loved ones in the future
3. Organizing a lifetime of photos
4. Making photo slideshows for memorials
5. Distributing gifts (jewellery, special items)
6. Managing social media posts
7. Establishing a vigil routine for the final days or hours
8. Setting up a spiritual shrine and chanting prayers

Holding the Space

Speech is not just involved with the words we choose to use, but it includes the way we use the words. In 2015, Heather Plett, a writer and facilitator from Winnipeg, Manitoba, wrote a blog on the topic of "holding the space".[31] Her blog went viral,

---

31 Plett, H. (March 11, 2015). *What it means to "hold space" for people, plus eight tips on how to do it well.* heatherplett.com

crashed her website, and this phrase burst out from the language of yoga practitioners and began being used as the quintessential way to describe being around death. She describes "holding the space" as being "willing to walk alongside another person in whatever journey they're on without judging them, making them feel inadequate, trying to fix them, or trying to impact the outcome. When we hold space for other people, we open our hearts, offer unconditional support, and let go of judgment and control."

Heather describes eight lessons she has learned from being with her own mom who was dying, as well as from other people who have held space for her. They can be summarized as not trying to fix anything, but just being with it as it is. Many of these lessons apply not just at end of life, but in other tough life situations that require more acceptance and less fixing.

1. Give people permission to trust their own intuition and wisdom.
2. Give people only as much information as they can handle.
3. Don't take their power away.
4. Keep your own ego out of it.
5. Make them feel safe enough to fail.
6. Give guidance and help with humility and thoughtfulness.
7. Create a container for complex emotions (fear, trauma, etc.).
8. Allow them to make different decisions and to have different experiences than you would.

☙

People are natural storytellers. Doing a life review at the end is an excellent way to think back on all the decisions and people and stories that made a life. On the one hand, it is super helpful to focus on one day at a time as life closes in on death, and do whatever feels right for that day. On the other hand, a life is long, and it's comforting to tell old stories. Go back to pivotal moments like when the dying person fell in love, when they decided to take the career they took, or when they achieved a milestone. Invite them to share whatever stories they want to share and remember, or tell your own. Stories bring the whole life into perspective, and allow for self-acceptance and letting go of things previously held to that really don't matter.

Speech will be extremely important until it's not. Until it's too hard to focus on the conversation. Until you can't really hear voices. Until you start disconnecting and no longer really care about this lifetime. This transition can be unsettling for a loved one to watch, but it's helpful to know that it is normal. In fact, it's the human organism's way of dying – to let go of attachments to this life. It's not uncommon to become more interested in professional staff taking care of you than your spouse who cared for you for 40 years. This is simply the easier way to let go of who and what you have been, and to move on into the next lifetime.

Speech at 21 Days

Some people are conscious, responsive, and communicative up to the final minutes, while others spend weeks in unresponsive states. There is no explanation or prediction in this regard. It's not about introvert or extrovert. If there are words to be spoken aloud, say them before it's too late.

For many dying people, the final 21 days are mostly quiet. Focus is on the internal process of dying. The effort of carrying on a conversation is too much. There may still be occasional words, but with little food and drink, there is also little energy. Words may be few and far between. The pace to speak and answer is slow.

Hopefully, all the final words have been spoken, and there can be an ease in sitting together quietly. Practical conversations about the old life, like wishes for the house or garden, no longer matter. Even funeral arrangements or meeting with a lawyer are of no concern to the dying.

This can be a lonely time for the caregiver, because the body is still living but the sense of personhood is already slipping away. It's important to have support for caregivers and respite, and ideally more than one person sitting at a time. As we discovered in the research, at PPS of 10, the speech needs of the caregiver are more important than the dying person, who is more likely content in their own world, which is about to slip away when PPS drops to 0.

4

Mind at End of Life

Much of what we think of as "me" is our concept of "mind". It includes body and speech, but it is mind that holds it all together. According to the Buddhist concept of "self" or ego, we are really only a conglomerate of five parts or "aggregates" – feelings, thoughts, perceptions, mental formations, and consciousness. In the same way, a car is only a conglomerate of a metal frame, four tires, two bumpers, lights, breaks, engine, windshields, and a host of other smaller components. When a car loses one of these components, it is still a car. But at some point, if you keep taking away parts, what is left is no longer a car. One might say that when it loses a key component such as tires or engine, it can no longer function as a car, even though it might still look like a car. An old wreck sitting in a farmer's field might still be called a car, but one does not expect to use it to drive into town.

In the same way, a person is still a person all through the dying process. But at some point, they are no longer a person. They are just a body. To be disposed of in some way. What is that point when they cross over from person to body? Does it happen all at once? Or is it like a car that slowly loses its components until it is no longer a car. Does breath define one as a person? Is it consciousness? Do mind and body disappear or transition together?

Losses

If you observe the dying process, you notice that there are many losses along the way. Sometimes these are called "cascading losses", because one loss flows into another in the stream of life. They are never-ending. Some are noisy and big, and others are seemingly small. Some losses, such as travelling less, are connected to the aging process, but cannot be separated from the dying process when they become even more extreme.

Understanding the dying process requires one to recognize the importance of these losses and the impact they have on one's sense of identity. Some people might say that one loss is too many. Others might be willing to lose or give up a number of things in exchange for a few primary components of self. Remembering how hard it is to lose something is helpful in being patient with the dying person when they resist yet one more loss.

Here is a list of common losses that a dying person experiences, in no particular order. They are listed in no particular order because life is not orderly, and neither is death. Some losses can be deliberately chosen as to timing, while others are ripped out of us:

- Working
- Driving a car or bicycle
- Travelling
- Hobbies
- Feeling well
- Looking good
- Ability to speak in native language or "recent" language ability
- Being social and connected
- Using the toilet alone
- Caring about the future

Advanced Care Planning

An Advanced Care Plan (ACP) is one way for the dying person to tell friends and family what matters to them. It is a written statement of their values and how they want to guide you or their designated power of attorney to make treatment decisions for them when they are no longer competent to do so. (Advanced Care Plans are called Living Wills in the United States, and they have a different legal status than Canadian ones.) The paperwork for ACPs varies by province, and there is a great website that includes links to each one.[32] These plans can all be downloaded for free from the website, or a paper version can be sent to a mailing address. It is important to have the correct form for the province or territory for where the dying person is located at end of life.

ACPs seem daunting, but really, they boil down to some basic questions. Here are the Ontario questions that are typical of questions in other provinces as well:

1. What do I value most in terms of my mental and physical health?
2. What would make prolonging life unacceptable for me?
3. When I think about death, what are the things I worry about happening?
4. If I were nearing death, what would I want to make the end more peaceful for me?
5. What are the spiritual or religious beliefs that would affect my care at the end of life?

ACPs are not legal documents in Canada, and do not need to be notarized or completed by lawyers. There is NO COST involved in completing one, so no one

---

32 Speak Up. advancecareplanning.ca

can use cost as reason to avoid them. There are different versions that you might find on different websites that you find better describes your wishes than the standard ones, and this is ok. If the dying person needs help thinking about the questions and various options, the book *Being Mortal: Medicine and What Matters Most* by Dr. Atul Gawande[33] is a great place to start. He writes about these questions of quality of life as they apply to the dying process and treatment options and how his family applied his father's wishes written in an ACP.

ACPs are directives, and not treatment plans. It is impossible to think of all the possible scenarios that might come up in life, so a good ACP is more general than specific. ACPs give a sense of what is important for quality of life, and how one balances this with quantity of life.

The Covid-19 pandemic has increased the urgency for many elderly people who now recognize that life can change quickly with a virus, and advanced care directives must be in place long before a crisis. It has also made people rethink their quality-of-life criteria regarding treatment that buys them additional time but requires them to live out their lives in long-term care homes. Seeing how badly many are run, and the staffing shortages inherent in the current funding of these homes (particularly the privately-owned homes), many people are questioning treatment choices that keep them alive and requiring such long-term care.

The most important thing to know about ACPs is that filling in the form is just the beginning. ACPs need to be shared and turned into a conversation between the dying person and the people chosen to be the Power of Attorney (for personal care) or Substitute Decision Maker. In fact, it's best to share the ACP with all the loved ones as well as with doctors, so everyone knows in advance how the dying person will be approaching the dying process. One might say this requires a fearlessness of death for both the dying person and their caregivers, and I would agree. And that is what this book is all about. It is about providing the caregiver with necessary knowledge and inviting them to talk to the dying person about these questions well in advance of needing to act on these plans.

My personal wish is that every single Canadian over the age of 18 has a completed Advanced Care Plan. If they need help understanding their values, the role of a helper to complete ACPs can be played by family doctors, social workers, nurses, and even lawyers (this is an expensive way, and not necessarily one that uses their best skills and training). There are many people out there willing to discuss these hard questions together. One of my good friends, Dr. Julie McIntyre, has retired from her work as a family doctor, and has dedicated her remaining years to talking to people about the importance of ACPs. She is a calm and informed presence who will accompany anyone into their own fear of death and bring them out the other side with completed plans and an acceptance of their own decisions.

---

33 Gawanda, A. (2014). *Being Mortal: Medicine and What Matters in the End.*

I've found helping people with Advance Care Planning an extremely rewarding occupation. It involves exploring their values, wishes, and beliefs and how these can be used to direct the medical care they would want if they become seriously ill or are dying and cannot speak for themselves. Not surprisingly, research indicates that there is less depression and prolonged grief among the bereaved of individuals who had Advance Care Plans. There is also evidence that individuals with ACPs are more likely to die where and how they would prefer.

Dr. Julie McIntyre, Advanced Care Planning and End of Life Counselling

If ACPs tell us what one wants, then the next question is who one trusts to implement those wishes. For people who refuse to plan their dying process, the government steps in to present a list of who is considered to be the most trusted implementer. This role is known as the Substitute Decision Maker, or SDM. The SDM is the person who will be asked to step up to make a health or personal care decision when the sick or dying person is unable to do so. There are slight variations between the provinces, but this is the Ontario ranked order:

Substitute Decision Making Hierarchy

SUBSTITUTE DECISION MAKER HIERARCY
Legally appointed SDMs
Court Appointed Guardian
Attorney for Personal Care
Representative appointed by Consent and Capacity Board
Automatic family member SDMs
Spouse or Partner
Parents or Children
Parent with right of access only
Any other relative
SDM of last resort
Public Guardian and Trustee
Ontario's *Health Care Consent Act*, 1996

(Left margin, vertical: ▼ Decreasing order of authority)

If the dying person likes this ranking, they don't need to do anything, because it is the default. But if they disagree with it, then they must plan ahead and complete paperwork clarifying whom they choose instead. If there is more than one person on a given line, then ALL those people must be involved and agree. This can be very cumbersome, and it's usually better to narrow down the list to two people, either of whom have authority to make a decision, with the idea that they would consult for decisions together if time allowed.

There was a time when it was assumed that one's spouse was the best *SDM* in all cases, but court cases and family conflict have proven that dying people and their spouses have inherently differing needs and spouses often deliberately go against wishes. After completing ACPs, it's helpful to have a conversation between the dying person and the proposed SDM to determine the SDM's willingness to implement the ACP, especially the wishes that go against the SDM's wishes. In such cases, it may be better to designate a different person as SDM.

To choose a different decision-maker from the default SDM list, one must complete Power of Attorney forms for healthcare. A POA form does not need to be authorized by a lawyer, but simply needs to be signed by witnesses. However, sometimes lawyers who complete financial wills will recommend getting the POA authorized by a lawyer as well, if there is any possibility of a family debate or conflict over your choice. POA forms can be found for each province on the same Canadian website that has the ACP forms – www.advancecareplanning.ca.

There are also POA forms for designating who will handle finances when the dying person is no longer capable. This authorization is only while the dying person is still alive, and as soon as they die, then the executor takes over finances. Sometimes these are different people, and sometimes they will be the same person. While it's good to choose a financial POA and complete forms ahead of time, a bank will often require up-to-date signed forms before they accept someone else's financial authority. In many cases, it is easier to release oneself from all financial commitments before one loses mental capacity. This includes ownership of vehicles, names on bank accounts (make them joint accounts), and release from mortgages or deeds. This release is not only beneficial for your executor, but it's also a symbolic release of mind that allows death to be more natural and easeful, and is therefore highly recommended.

Advanced Care Planning is made hard by our collective denial of death. Yvonne Heath is a nurse in Ontario who stopped practicing direct care after 27 years so she could move full time into public education, challenging the way most people approach grief and death. She wrote a book called *Love Your Life to Death*[34] and travels extensively promoting the book and encouraging open conversations about death. She is one of the new voices suggesting heart and even humour in her approach to this often-heavy message. She is very passionate about helping people understand and recognize grief as it shows up throughout life, not just at end of life, and for showing how grief and joy can co-exist.

Her message is always important, but is even more relevant now as more and more Canadians are succumbing unexpectedly to death during the Covid-19 pandemic. Too many people have been caught off guard assuming they had more

34 Heath, Y. (2015). *Love Your Life to Death.*

years to live. My heart goes out to all the families who had loved ones who caught the virus, struggled at home, and then called 911 in a crisis and never saw each other again. The collective grief of this experience will continue to roll out, and I worry that we will have a tsunami of complex grief for some time.

> Because we don't have a deadline (pun intended) we pretend we
> will have time to prepare for end of life. But we do not all die of old
> age and we do not always get a warning. Do it now!
> *Yvonne Heath, Speaker, Author, and Changemaker*

If you're worried about all these forms and the organization of it all, you might be interested in Purchasing Karry Sawatsky's book – *Modern Deathcare End-of-Life Planning Guide.*[35] This is a fill-in-the-blank made-in-Canada guide that pulls together all your end-of-life wishes in one book and helps guide your conversations.

Hope

As people get closer to dying, there is a lot of talk about hope. It always bugs me. Hope is often described like a light switch – either someone has hope, or they don't have hope. There's no in-between. And also, the statement of hope without an object doesn't seem to me to be grammatically correct. Hope for what? It sounds to my ears like a half-finished sentence to say one has hope (or one has lost hope, like it is a glove or sock or something). When I hear talk of hope, I feel compelled to stop and ask what the hope is for. It seems that hope requires an object. A something. I can understand if someone says they hope they don't die this week. Or they hope that their brother visits before they die. Too often, hope is so open-ended that it simply means nothing. And in these cases, it sounds like hoping that there will be no death.

This unfinished sentence about hope may be fragile and sensitive. In my work as a social worker at a hospice, I have been asked twice to leave a family conversation. Both times were because I dove into conversations about hope, and these two families did not welcome it at the time. This was perhaps a "skill in means" issue, in that I had the right intention, but did not execute it well. I leaned in where others avoided, and crossed over a line with these families. I judged them as ready to talk about death, and they were not yet ready. I was ahead of them about what was actually going on with their loved one, and they were not ready to go there with me. The first time, the dying person was in her 20s and her husband was angry, and understandably so. The other time, the dying person died within a few hours of our conversation, but that doesn't mean the parents were ready for it. Interestingly, both families eventually apologized (needlessly, from my perspective), but they

---

35 Sawatsky, K. *Modern Deathcare End of Life Planning Guide.* moderndeathcare.ca

both admitted they were just not ready to face their lack of hope that death would not come for their loved one.

It is also common for dying people to talk about wanting to go "home". This is easy to understand as a metaphorical "home" when dying persons are still at home, but when they are in hospital or hospice, it can get a little muddled. Family members often treat it literally, and consider whether to take them out of hospice and to try to handle their care needs at home again. However, it is better to listen to the deeper wish, as it is usually a sign of acceptance of impending death. Wishing to go home is a sign that the dying person has seen ahead past the death moment and accepted the reality. It reflects a deep knowing about the death process that they seemed to not have possessed before. Understanding this can be comforting to the family if they understand that it means acceptance. Not approval, just well-being in the acceptance of dying.

It is a common wish to hear dying people speak of "a wish to die". For people of a certain age, this is a commonly stated wish, often long before their own death. The dying person might have already attended plenty of funerals and memorial services, as well as losing important loved ones, and are just wanting to end the grieving phase. There is a tipping point when death is no longer personal and it just is. So wanting to die can mean the dying person is ready for their turn. This is especially common if the disease has taken so much away already and the quality of life is poor but the mind is still clear and lucid. It can be harder for a strong mind to watch the body decline than for a confused mind to watch the body decline.

The wish to die is not a suicidal wish, and as such does not require a suicide risk assessment. I have never seen or heard of a dying person ending their own life as they near the end, or even attempting such a thing. Suicidal ideation is a distorted thought that appears earlier in life to a mind that is suffering, and is not connected to the body dying.

The wish to die is also not usually a serious request for Medical Assistance in Dying. It should not be thought of as a wish that needs any action, other than a nod. When one wants action to hasten death, that desire is more clearly requested and follows a much greater protocol. The wish to die is an ancient statement of readiness that is exactly as it sounds – a wish. It is not a call to action.

Ethical Dilemmas

There are a number of ethical considerations that are related to decisions, as the dying person gets closer to death. Ethics includes three levels of consideration. Law – what we must do, Ethics – what we ought to do, and Policy – what we agree to do. These three aspects overlap and impact any end-of-life decisions that appear. One of the first decisions in the treatment phase will probably involve the use of opioids and pain medication. No matter the disease, pain is often (but not always!) a part of the body breaking down and dying. Good quality palliative care relies heavily on the use of opioids to manage pain. While over-the-counter pain medications like Tylenol and Advil work with life pain, they rarely touch death pain.

The most common opioid for death pain is Hydromorphone, a derivative of Morphine that is ten times as powerful as Morphine. It is called Dilaudid in other parts of the hospital, and is used to handle acute severe pain. Hydromorphone not only treats pain, but also treats breathing issues, another very common symptom in the final stages. It can be delivered orally in pill form, through a needle, or by pump directly into the body by subcutaneous drip (called "sub-q" in medical lingo). This flexibility makes it ideal for end-of-life treatment when swallowing gets hard. Family members at home can be trained to administer all forms of Hydromorphone, including the pain pump with a button for fast acting relief. There are other opioid pain medications - Codeine, Oxycontin, and Fentanyl - that might also be used, particularly if Morphine or Hydromorphone aren't effective. Sometimes other classes of drugs, like those used for treating depression, inflammation, or seizure disorders are useful.

There are many myths and fears around the use of opioids. First, in the '80s, when palliative care was still developing, there was a myth that opioids caused problems with addiction when used for pain control, so opioids were prescribed in tiny doses that never touched the real pain. Much higher doses are allowed today, although levels still start small and pain and opioid quantity is better monitored. At end of life, the future of addiction is not as relevant.

Additionally, opioids were not given to anyone with a history of addictions, because there was a myth that addicts generally overrepresented their pain in order to get higher doses. Today, palliative care doctors understand that pain must be managed no matter the history of addictions, and that a history of addictions is generally not related to the severity of pain experienced.

Finally, there is a myth that many people receiving opioids for palliative pain control die of opioid overdose at end of life. People die of diseases. Opioids can hasten death slightly, but their purpose is to improve quality of life. Sometimes people die shortly after getting an opioid dose, but that is not the cause of death. The opioid may help them relax and let go into death, and their life may be shortened by hours or days, but if they aren't ready, they won't die. The little bit of extra opioid is unlikely to cause death if the person wasn't already close to end of life. Let's stop giving opioids the credit by saying that people die from an overdose. Let's name the disease that takes the life.

You might have read that Canada is experiencing an opioid crisis. The situation was terribly dangerous before the Covid-19 pandemic, and it has only gotten worse. However, that is about street use of opioids and not end of life use. Street use often involves Fentanyl and Carfentanyl, a synthetic opioid that is 100 times more potent than Fentanyl, and 10,000 times more potent than Morphine. The opioid crisis is a problem because dosage is not easily controllable when substances are mixed and interchanged. The opioid crisis in Canada is not related to the regulated use of opioids by doctors who prescribe and monitor doses precisely for pain at end of life. Unfortunately, sometimes opioids for end of life get diverted into street use.

@

People have different views of what is happening in the final days and moments of life, and also what comes after the final breath. These views are often determined by religious and spiritual beliefs about what happens after the last breath. These views will shape the values and what is considered most important for that life. Sometimes symptom relief for the body is most important. Sometimes clarity of mind is most important. Sometimes the comfort of the caregivers is most important. These values will show up in illness situations earlier in life. If the dying person is someone who reaches for a pill for every body ailment earlier in life, they might make similar choices at end of life. If they have avoided pills and chosen herbal remedies, meditation, or stoicism of mind, they will likely make similar choices at end of life.

I've heard women say that the way they chose to deliver their babies was similar to how they ultimately chose to die. If they wanted an epidural and anaesthetic for birth, they will likely want lots of opioid use at death. If this is true, I will be facing my own death by having a party with lots of friends and family of all ages around me at my home with a "natural death" like my "natural birth".

The Buddhist view of opioids is strongly influenced by the edict to have as clear a mind as possible in order to be able to choose the best rebirth. This view is of lesser importance in other religions, but may still show up in other spiritual beliefs that include expectations of an afterlife. A clear mind allows for spiritual practice during end of life, considered to be the most influential spiritual moment of one's lifetime according to Buddhist texts. Of course, one's whole life also matters for merit, but Buddhist texts and practices are consistent in their emphasis on death as an opportunity. Most Buddhist teachers would say this does not necessarily preclude *any* opioid use, as low doses may actually make for a clearer mind. An ardent Buddhist might try other options for reducing pain and shortness of breath issues before turning to opioids, or using as low a dose as possible to handle the pain.

Ironically, there is an idea called "staying ahead of the pain", which means treating pain with smaller doses on a regular basis that allows for fewer spikes in pain, and ultimately fewer breakthrough large doses, a lower drowsiness factor and greater mind clarity overall. This may demonstrate the modern version of the "Buddhist Middle Way" which calls for moderation, but not necessarily renunciation of all use of opioids. In fact, pain and suffering can reduce clear mind as much or more than moderate opioid use.

In most cases, a moderate amount of opioid use will address pain issues and dying people can now expect to be able to handle the pain of dying. However, sometimes pain just can't be managed. Remember that Dame Cicely Saunders coined the phrase "total pain", to identify four sources of pain at end of life – physical, social, psychological/emotional, and spiritual. Opioid use will really only address the physical pain, so if the other sources are present, the pain might persist. It's not realistic to think that opioids will take away the other pain, or guarantee no pain at end of life.

Buddhists accept that all of life is about suffering. Dying is thought to be no different. So if there is suffering that appears in the dying process, perhaps the relationship to the pain can be observed and be a thing to study rather than something to remove. Andrew Holecek, an American teacher in Bardo Studies, which look at end of life stages, encourages finding acceptance of the pain, rather than pushing it away and denying it, which ironically often makes it worse. He describes this as: *Suffering = Pain x Resistance.*[36]

In other words, pain exists, and we create more suffering when we add resistance to that pain. If we want to reduce the suffering, we can remove or reduce the resistance. We do not require pain medication to remove all the suffering. It's a matter of the mind. Suffering is temporary and we might try to accept dying suffering as necessary suffering.

If the primary goal of limiting medications in general is to choose the ones with the least sedating qualities, then one category to try to avoid might be the anti-anxiety medications, in particular Haldol. This medication treats terminal agitation and delirium, but can also cause heavy sedation and confusion. It is more likely to sedate and decrease the clear mind than any of the opioids, which may sedate initially, but not after adjusting to the dose. There is also a sense that anxiety about death may be better dealt with non-medicinally through talking with a social worker, spiritual teacher, or directly with family members.

✲

There are also new methods coming out that help address fear of death. New research shows hope that a single dose of psilocybin ("magic mushrooms" or "shrooms") might relieve anxiety induced by cancer and other end of life declines.[37] I have also successfully used EMDR (Eye Movement Desensitization and

---

36 Holecek, A. (2013). *Preparing to Die: Practical Advice and Spiritual Wisdom from the Tibetan Spiritual Tradition.*

37 Ross, S., Bossis, A., Guss, J., Agin-Liebes, G., Malone, T., Cohen, B., Mennenga, S. E., Belser, A., Kalliontzi, K., Babb, J., Su, Z., Corby, P., & Schmidt, B. L. (2016). Rapid and sustained symptom reduction following psilocybin treatment for anxiety and depression in patients with life-threatening cancer: a randomized controlled trial. *Journal of psychopharmacology (Oxford, England), 30*(12), 1165–1180.

Reprocessing) Psychotherapy[38] to address fear of death with people prior to dying. EMDR works by identifying the negative memory that caused the generation of a Negative Cognition related to Safety, Faulty Responsibility, or Control. The EMDR session then treats this memory with bilateral stimulation of touch, sight, or sound to reprocess the memory and release the emotional trauma. By working in the field of dying and death and pushing to provide services to dying people earlier and further upstream from end of life, I hope that there might one day be a recognition of the need to address fear of death sooner and with non-medicinal treatments.

Palliative Sedation

For pain that cannot be managed by opioids, one option that might be offered may be palliative sedation. For persons who have never heard of this treatment option, I suggest you view the film *Wit*,[39] starring Emma Thompson. It is clearly a Hollywood film, but it does a good job of personalizing it and describing what it looks like and why someone might choose it.

Palliative sedation is described as aiming "to relieve intolerable suffering from refractory symptoms by the intentional lowering of a patient's level of consciousness in the last days of life by the proportional and monitored use of non-opioid sedative medications."[40] It is achieved with the use of a pain pump, and requires constant monitoring by a registered nurse, so cannot usually be achieved at home. Once it has begun, there is usually no going back to full consciousness again.

Palliative sedation doesn't hasten death per se, but people receiving palliative sedation also stop eating and drinking for safety sake, so death tends to come quickly, but this is not officially the intended consequence. In other words, palliative sedation often hastens death a bit, but this is not its primary purpose, and so it is still considered a palliative care treatment option. It is an important part of palliative care, to be used when pain or fear of dying cannot be adequately managed any other way. It is important not to feel guilty if that's what you want. Sometimes just knowing this option is available gives people peace of mind not to use it.

People who aspire to clarity of mind at end of life would not usually support the choice of palliative sedation. Palliative sedation tends to create a lack of awareness, which is the opposite of the clear mind aspiration. Palliative sedation is not something that is usually recommended for any particular disease, but is more about one's psychological state, and in particular one's anxiety related to fear of death. If one can face death directly, and not be overwhelmed with the psychological

38 EMDR. *What is EMDR?* emdria.org

39 Nichols, M. (Director) (2001). *WIT* [Film].

40 Fraser Health (2011). *Refractory Symptoms and Palliative Sedation Therapy Guideline.* fraserhealth.ca

issues, one can usually manage the pain sufficiently through other methods without choosing palliative sedation.

> Samantha was admitted to the hospice as a 33-year-old, dying of congenital heart disease. She also had a developmental delay, and didn't really understand fully her situation. She had been told she was at risk for dying since she was born, and her mother had lived with this. As she was taken off her life-sustaining medications, it was expected she would die within a few days. After two weeks of continuing to live, she couldn't handle the death anxiety that arose for her. She had limited capacity for understanding and she was angry and irritable all the time. Numerous kinds of pain management were tried, but nothing worked to reduce her death anxiety. Eventually her mother requested palliative sedation to provide a calm way for her to accept her dying. She was never completely sedated or unconscious, but the treatment allowed her to calmly die, three days after beginning the palliative sedation.

Medical Assistance in Dying

The most contentious ethical dilemma for Canadians at end of life involves the choice of Medical Assistance in Dying, or MAiD, as it's called. On June 6, 2016, MAiD became legal across Canada. For the first time, dying Canadians became eligible to request a doctor or nurse practitioner to give a lethal prescription by mouth or IV to end their life. This intervention can be done in a home, residential hospice, or hospital. There are very specific eligibility requirements and guidelines for doctors.

Eligibility:
- Be at least 18 years of age
- Be eligible for publicly-funded healthcare in Canada
- Be able to give consent throughout the process
- Have a "grievous and irremediable" medical condition
- Be suffering intolerably from this condition
- Be in an advanced state of decline
- Be at the point where natural death is foreseeable
- Make a request of your own free will[41]

In the first 3.5 years after legalizing this intervention, there were 13,946 MAiD deaths. While the number of MAiD deaths is increasing year over year, and in all

---

41 Government of Canada: Health Services (July 24, 2020). *First Annual Report on Medical Assistance in Dying in Canada, 2019.* canada.ca

the provinces, this is only 2% of total deaths in Canada.[42] Palliative Care doctors are often conflicted about whether to support MAiD, as the definition of palliative care specifically *excludes* the hastening of death, which MAiD most certainly does. Likewise, most residential hospices in Ontario have policies that exclude the MAiD intervention, and screen for this at the intake. Hospices that are willing to have the MAiD intervention done onsite are often larger organizations that have fuller senior services including Long Term Care Homes, like the Margaret Bahen Hospice in Newmarket, affiliated with the massive Better Living Health and Community Services agency.

Other provinces, like British Columbia, have insisted that MAiD be included as an option at residential hospices receiving public funding. As a result of this, the Irene Thomas Hospice in Delta, BC, has decided to lay off staff and to move closer to closing its doors in February, 2021. They have decided to decline all funding in response to this new requirement and no longer operate, rather than agreeing to offer MAiD.[43]

In Canada, MAiD is usually delivered by the administration of three medications in an IV. For this reason, most people choose to do this intervention in a hospital, as there is more support and control there compared to a home, or hospice. This is in contrast to the practice in many American states, like Oregon, where the doctor gives the patient a prescription for an oral medication.

As I write this book in early 2021, there are proposed changes to the MAiD legislation being hotly debated. They include the opening up of several requirements, namely: 1) whether a natural death is reasonably foreseeable; 2) allowing for a request to be carried out even if the person loses capacity (from the dying process or dementia). Despite strong debate, two issues that are *not* being considered in the latest update is the inclusion of people suffering solely from mental illness and mature minors.[44]

Buddhists generally do not approve of MAiD, because the lethal dose of medication needed to be effective to end life necessarily clouds the mind. In fact, there is only a brief 15 minutes that it takes from the starting of the IV to the stopping of the heart, and while it looks peaceful to onlookers, the mind of the dying person is unable to do any spiritual practice under these conditions. Buddhists and others might show compassion to those who decide their suffering is so great that they choose this option, as it is everyone's choice how they choose to die. The doctor who chooses to perform this intervention probably is not concerned with "Right Livelihood", the fourth step on the Eightfold Noble Path. Previous examples of live-

---

42 Ibid.

43 Kane, L. (2021, January 8). Government of Canada: Department of Justice Canada. (October 5, 2020). *Government of Canada reintroduces proposed changes to medical assistance in dying legislation.* canada.ca

44 Layoffs at B.C. hospice that refused to offer medical assistance in dying (January 8, 2021). *Toronto Star.* thestar.com

lihood excluded from good choices for Right Livelihood included butchers, funeral directors, and street sweepers, and would likely include MAiD doctors. Other religions may also not approve of the MAiD choice, with the most vocal of these being the Catholic doctors at Catholic hospitals. This is a divisive issue, as doctors advocate for religious freedoms, while hospitals receive public funding and are obligated to adhere to laws of Canada.

I have had several interesting experiences working with dying people considering MAiD for themselves. On three occasions, I have had conversations about MAiD with people in hospice who requested I notify doctors of their request for it, only to have them take a quick turn into unresponsiveness making them ineligible for MAiD within 24 hours before ever talking with the doctor about it. It appears as if the work it takes for the mind to make the decision to request MAiD is what it takes to let go and die, without even needing the lethal injection.

> Mariyam was diagnosed with colon cancer at the age of 42. She came to me for psychotherapy in my private practice because she didn't feel like she was getting all the information and support she wanted from her oncologist. I supported her making one last trip to Arizona to soak in some warmth. I encouraged her to ask her oncologist for a prognosis at one point, and she was given 4-6 more months. She didn't think she could handle this and asked me to explain MAiD to her, which I did. I went on vacation for two weeks. By the time I returned, she had died. A few days after our last conversation, she had requested MAiD from her doctor, but then crashed two days later, and had died before she could get close to activating the request and even signing forms. I spoke with her husband who said it was a peaceful death and she had been relieved to die so quickly.

In truth, even with MAiD one must make peace with death. MAiD does not give a detour around this work. It speeds death up a bit, sometimes weeks or months, and in some ways, it requires a greater fearlessness to request a slightly early death. In fact, because there is a 10-day waiting period built into the current process, one must still wait for death.

The most common reason for requesting MAiD is to prevent suffering down the road. For many people, the dying process is too slow. It is long and painful, particularly with some neurological diseases like ALS or Parkinson's. Most people want to die quickly, often within a month of being ready. The final weeks can be hard. Because few people recognize the final 21 days, they don't know when they will naturally have less than a month till death. And their caregivers and the care team are not telling them, either because they don't know, or because they assume that the dying person doesn't want to know. If more people recognized when dying people were only 21 days from death, there would likely be fewer people asking for MAiD. And if we had more caregivers trained to properly support their loved ones, these final 21 days would be more precious and not worth skipping and avoiding.

Organ Donation

Another ethical dilemma concerning the body at death is the issue of organ donation. Organ donation in Canada is mostly an opt-in consideration, but it is one that must be decided quickly. Medical centres will often ask families about organ donation, if the death is sudden, and particularly if the dying person was young and healthy. Persons over the age of 50 are not often asked to be donors, as their body parts have aged too much to be worth the risk of transfer. The most common organ donations in Canada are kidney, liver, heart, lung, pancreas, small intestine, eye, bone, skin, and heart valve.[45]

Organ donation is still a relatively new consideration. The first organ donation and transplant in Canada was a kidney in 1954.[46] Since then, many more organs have been successfully transplanted. Organ donation varies by country, with many Asian countries holding the belief that organ donation combines people in funny ways, and they do not culturally support the notion. One of the systemic issues holding down numbers of organ donation is that most jurisdictions have an opt-in requirement, and often things move too fast at point of death to make it possible. In January, 2021, Nova Scotia became the first jurisdiction in North American to presume that adults are willing to donate their organs when they die, with other regions not far behind.[47]

Organ donation requires disturbing the physical body during the first four to 24 hours after death. This is the death phase of the Bardos (0-72 hours), and is the most spiritually important time, according to Buddhists. In the Jewish faith practice of Shemira, a guard accompanies the body from time of death until burial, as it is thought that the human soul is confused between death and burial. They also believe that the soul hovers over the body for either 3 or 7 days, and could be disturbed with organ donation. In Islamic beliefs, the body is expected to be buried as quickly as possible after death, often within 12-24 hours, making it difficult to harvest organs within this time frame. Islamic faith also asserts that the body needs to be respected in death as in life, and not cut or harmed in any unnecessary way, as might be needed to be done for an organ donation. In truth, in Canada the body regularly gets disturbed during this time, as bodies are shuffled quickly out of

45 Trillium Gift of Life Network. giftoflife.on.ca

46 McGill University Health Centre celebrates 50th anniversary of Canada's 1st kidney transplant News (October 2, 2008). *McGill University Health Center.* mcgill.ca/channels

47 Ray, C. (January 18, 2021). One person dies, another lives. *CBC News.* newsinteractives.cbc.ca

hospital rooms to make space for the next living person, and stored in a hospital morgue in the basement while awaiting pickup from a transport service. All this, regardless whether there is any organ donation or not.

Most Buddhists in Canada support organ donation as a useful civic contribution. They generally believe that the Bodhisattva Vow of being of service to others generally supports organ donation by balancing the karmic disruption in the death Bardo with the merit of saving a life. Other religions have similar beliefs around the contribution to saving lives through sharing organs. As hospitals provide better emotional support to families in making this decision and the surgeons increase the success rate of organ donation, the number of donations is slowly increasing in Canada. Overall, organ donations have increased by 59% in Canada in the last ten years, with hopes for even more in the years ahead.[48]

Suicide

A final ethical dilemma is the debate about suicide, and whether this has any lasting impact for the individual or society. It is easy to assert that suicide is never an easy choice for anyone, and we can assume that it is not the desired choice either. People who suicide feel a hopelessness that most of us will never comprehend. It is a state of mind that cannot see any other way out of the intense suffering. I feel a deep compassion toward anyone who wanders into this state, and wish that we could find a way to identify in advance the mind that contemplates suicide, and also ensure a way to properly support this mind to see alternatives.

Language around suicide has changed. We have stopped referring to it as "committing suicide", as the verb "to commit" implies an illegal action. Suicide has not been a criminal offense in Canada since 1972.[49] New language refers to suicide saying that a person has suicided, or that someone has ended their life by suicide. We have a long way to go before we, as a society, can talk openly about suicide, but it helps if we start by using more accurate and inclusive language.

No religion looks kindly at people who take their own lives. There may be individuals who consider it a legitimate choice, but all religions see it as hindering options for the afterlife. People who suicide and end their own life interrupt their natural karma in a negative way. Nowhere in the Bible does it explicitly forbid suicide, but both Jewish and Christian leaders tend to interpret numerous scriptures as offering prohibitions against it. For Sikhs, suicide is an interference in God's plan for birth and death, and after suicide you must continue to carry out consequences and redemption in the afterlife, until finally you are released. In Buddhism, it is thought that people who suicide and "squander" their human life will not be given

---

48 Canadian Institute for Health Information. *Organ donor rates.* cihi.ca

49 Kellner, F. (2020). *Suicide in Canada.* thecanadianencyclopedia.ca

another human life again in the next rebirth. For these many reasons, all efforts should be made by everyone not to judge the mind that sees no alternatives, but rather to support people who are suffering and prevent suicide as much as we collectively can, given the negative karma shared by all.

Mind at 21 Days

We do not know exactly what is happening to the mind in the final 21 days, but we have some good guesses. The mind appears to be slipping in and out of consciousness in this lifetime and into the gap that prepares one for the next stage. Looking at the eyes, even the untrained caregiver can see that sometimes their loved one is in the room and sometimes they are gone. There may be different words to describe where they go, but the eyes look vacant and there is no potential for communication when this happens.

The final 21 days can be hard on the caregiver. They may already miss the dying person, and sense their absence. Whether it's a personal or a professional relationship, the separation can already be palpable. There may be little left to do at this point, and after months or years of active care, this reality may be hard to adjust to. The next phase is not quite happening, but it's close. The waiting is truly a hard place, and wishes for a reprieve and to see the end can feel so strange and anticlimactic.

Leaning into any spiritual practice for both the dying person and the caregiver can be a great relief in the final 21 days. It can be a thing to do together on behalf of the dying person, but also as a way to find peace and comfort for the caregiver.

5

Final 24-48 hours

The final 21 days brings many changes to the body, speech, and mind of the dying person, as described in the earlier chapters. The essence of the person has already slipped away. The dying person in front of you no longer resembles the loved one you once knew. For many, the visual image of the dying person is unsettling, with the open mouth and focus on breathing. But there is a great transition happening.

For many families, it is a relief to turn a loved one over to a hospital or residential hospice to take over the care, as the body breaks down and needs even more care than during the passive dying stage. However, when active dying begins, it is a time for the family and friends to again stay close and pour on the involvement, because time is short.

It is common to believe that what matters most is the final moment of life. Families often have strong opinions about who wants to be there for the final breath. The loved one has hopefully been invited to speak about how they imagine their ending, and whether they prefer to let go and die on their own, or be accompanied by a particular person or group.

The final 24-48 is called the active dying stage, and this is the time for the vigil. A vigil is often thought of as the 24/7 watch for death to arrive. For loved ones who live further away or have busier schedules and would like to arrive for the last breath, now is the time to call for these people.

During these final hours, I tell family members to consciously leave the room imagining that each time it may be the last. I don't mean just leaving the property, but even to go down the hall to use the washroom. Or if someone wants to go home to sleep, to do it mindfully and with love, in case that might be the last interaction.

Signs of Death

In this dying process, there is a point when death is imminent and the final stage of life appears. There are numerous names for this stage. Some call it "the turning". Others call it "the active dying phase". Time may have moved slowly in the previous several weeks or months, but at this stage the end is obviously near, even to people with little death education. There are distinct changes that make this stage apparent to anyone who wants to recognize it. Palliative Care Nurses, Social Workers, or Death Doulas easily recognize this stage. In fact, caregivers or anyone with an open mind can learn to recognize this stage. Experienced professionals will usually share this recognition with anyone they think is open to hearing it. This is the final stop on the runaway train we call the dying process.

Breathing Changes: Breath is the thing that distinguishes a living person from a dead person, so it makes sense that breathing changes are the most significant indications that death is drawing near. When the dying person turns toward death, the breathing rate changes. Mostly it slows down. Also, the breathing depth changes and becomes noticeably shallow.

Breathing patterns change, and they move between very slow and super rapid, with periods of apnea *up to a minute.* If you have never timed a minute, try it some time. It is a really long time to wait between breaths. People attending the vigil will be sure that the breathing has stopped completely. And then there is one more breath. And another looooong pause again. This apnea can occasionally go on for days, although often it's only hours.

The muscles used to breath at this time are different from normal. Instead of simply the diaphragm, the front of the neck and shoulders are used to lift the body up and breath in and out. It can make the person look like they are "struggling to breathe". If in doubt, check with nurses, but this is common, and almost always nothing to worry about. It is a different way of breathing, but it does not mean it is difficult to breathe.

The other breathing change that everyone knows about is the noisy breathing. Nurses call this "Terminal Secretions", but family members know it as the "Death Rattle". It is not painful or even annoying to the dying person, who is generally unresponsive by now, and we have no reason to think it disturbs them. The sound is caused when the dying person can no longer remove natural secretions of the mouth (like saliva), and this liquid vibrates on the vocal cords. There is a medication called Scopolamine that can be offered to dry up the secretions and remove the sound, but really it is a problem for the family, and not the dying person.

One of the other breathing changes to note is that sometime after the person fully dies, there are a few involuntary breaths. After watching apnea and pauses between breaths for so long, it can be odd to suddenly see a breath after the body has been pronounced dead by a nurse or doctor, but it is normal. It is not a sign of coming back to life, but merely a natural exhalation of the body removing its final air. One more final outbreath.

Consciousness changes: Dying is a process of the body, but also of the mind. The dying person typically sleeps more in the final days, even up to 23 hours a day. As the body shuts down, it is common to have more requests for pain medication. Extra medication may increase the confusion and disorientation of the mind, but even without medication, confusion is common. It is part of the dying process to remove one's consciousness from this world. Dying people often don't recognize loved ones in the room, or maybe they seem disconnected and out of the relationship already. And as mentioned in earlier chapters, dying people frequently talk to people not in the room, and sometimes to people who have already died.

People sometimes describe the dying person as being "unconscious". The dying process rarely makes a person unconscious. Consciousness can be measured using EKGs and CT scans, which determine whether the brain is able to register sensations. Unconsciousness is common following accidents and sudden trauma, but it's not common in the dying process. What looks like unconsciousness is actually an *unresponsive* state. This means the dying person is still alive in the brain and registering sensations, but they can no longer communicate with people in the room. For this reason, we remind caregivers to continue to communicate with loved ones by talking and touching, even if they appear not to respond or notice. There is plenty of evidence of people becoming responsive again and knowing what happened during unresponsive states.

> My friend tells the story of being with his 92-year-old grandmother in her final weeks. He loved her dearly, and visited her lots as she neared the end of her long and happy life. He brought his phone and passed the time with her playing old show tunes. As she slipped into unresponsiveness in her final week of life, others visited less, but he continued to visit and play music for her. One day when a different relative was with her, and after a week of unresponsiveness, she sat bolt upright in bed and asked for him by name, and mentioned that she'd appreciated the music he had been playing for her over the last few days. She died the next day, and the family recognized this as her final rally of lucidity. My friend was so grateful for the time he spent with her and that she had heard him.

Skin Changes: I am often struck by the fact that family members with no death education can intuitively notice signs of death. They understand that "mottling" – purple blotches on hands and feet – are a sign of something, even without being told what to look for. It is common to see nurses walk into a hospice room and nonchalantly remove blankets while providing medication to the dying person. I later learned that they were checking for signs of mottling, which they know only shows up in the final days.

Final hours often lead to checking the hands for white nails. As the body cools, blood pools in the extremities causing mottling, but it also fades from the fingers, leaving white fingers and nails. The skin becomes cool to the touch after days of warmth, sometimes even excess warmth.

Input/Output Changes: The dying process involves a close inspection of what goes in and what comes out. The analysis of these observations often guides the nurse's pronouncement of where the person is in the dying process. When little goes in but even less comes out, the end is imminent.

In the final hours, nearly all dying people will be classified as "NPO" – Latin for *nil per os* or nothing by mouth. I suggest remembering this as "nothing per oral" as most of us know little Latin. It means that the person cannot eat or drink, and can no longer even take medication orally or with applesauce.

While the body may not need water, the mouth is desperate for water and liquid all the way to the end. Therefore, a primary task of a caregiver in the final 48 hours is to assist with mouth care. Mouth care is the use of a toothette (sponge on a stick, like a popsicle) to transfer liquid to all parts of a dying person's mouth. This can be done hourly or more, depending on the disease and the level of discomfort. Water is most commonly used, but other liquids can be offered. Even if the person is NPO and cannot drink, they sometimes appreciate familiar or comforting tastes. If the dying person is responsive, you may ask what they prefer. If not, you may offer various tastes and see how they respond. Diluted mouthwash, either regular or the special Biotene brand, can be especially helpful.

> One of the common questions we are asked by family members at residential hospices is the rule concerning alcohol. I got used to describing it as the same as with any household – don't disturb the neighbours! One Scottish family brought their 86-year-old grandmother into the hospice. They told stories of what a jovial, social woman she'd always been, and how much she loved drinking Scotch. By this time, she was no longer eating, drinking, or speaking, but was fully conscious and still playful. I invited them to consider using a bit of Scotch on the toothette for mouthwash. They were happy to try, and delighted with the smile on this woman's face as she sucked the toothette!

The most common way to handle toileting needs in the final days is to insert a catheter to handle the urine. This is considerably easier on the dying person than trying to walk to a washroom or only wearing a brief (adult diaper) and needing to be changed regularly. Movement to a dying person can be painful and frankly impossible to handle. It is shocking how often the end of life comes immediately following a brief change. Therefore, a catheter is often used making it very easy to observe the output in the bag. Urine becomes darker and more concentrated as the kidneys shut down, and in the final hours, it is common for the urine to be very dark in colour and for there to be very little of it.

The Unexpected Rally

For dying people on various trajectories, there are ups and downs. However, in the final 21 days, it is usually down. The exception is the unexpected rally. After a number of "bad days", it is common to have one last good day. This may be for no expected reason, or it may align with a particular visit or a final large group gathering. Regardless of the reason, the person appears to be better. If they were unresponsive before, it is not unusual for the dying person to become responsive for a day or a few hours. During this time, they appear to have more energy again, and to even want to talk to certain people or say a few words, even if speaking is hard. Watching this, people want to believe the dying person is recovering. However, this is short-lived, and it passes, and often the dying person takes their last breath within 24 hours.

Unlike what happens in films, final moments are rarely filled with auspicious words. It is common for dying people to have been unresponsive for days or even weeks prior to the final moment. In fact, in my experience the most common final words spoken by dying people are about "peeing or pooing", two of the most important issues at end of life. So, if profound conversations are desired or craved for, don't wait till the end!

> Final conversations are unpredictable. At the residential hospice, I had a long discussion with a resident who had been debating whether to contact his estranged son as he neared the end of his own life. In this conversation, he had found peace with deciding not to contact his son. From this resolution, the conversation somehow went sideways and he asked me if I felt for him what he felt for me. I was confused, because he was married, 30 years older than me, and the earlier conversation had me thinking he was lucid. He went on to give me a proposal of love and marriage! I declined gently, and he died two hours later. Needless to say, I never shared this part of the conversation with his wife!

Final Days of Pain and Symptom Management

As death approaches, there are fewer things that need to be done. If the dying person sleeps more, keep visiting times brief or encourage visitors to sit quietly at the bedside. Plan conversation for when the person is more wakeful and alert. If the dying person's appetite has decreased, offer small servings of light food; decrease portions as the appetite decreases. Ask what would be preferred. Do not get upset if the meal isn't finished. If the patient has confusion and is unable to recognize familiar people or surroundings, tell the patient your name. Speak in a calm, natural tone. Remind the person of the time, place, and who is in the room. If the dying person experiences restlessness and pulling at bed linen/clothing, reassure the person and use gentle touch (avoid physical restraint). Soft, soothing music or gentle massage may ease restlessness.

Vigil

A vigil for the final hours can be either formal or informal, depending on the wishes of the dying person. For starters, there is the question of who the dying person wants to be there for their final breath. In my experience, this question is necessary to have with the dying person while they are still able to communicate their wishes, and indeed it should be based around the dying person's wishes. If I bring this topic up too soon, the dying person is not interested in answering the question. At the right moment, the dying person knows exactly what they want, and as I love to report, they *always* get what they want. If a dying person wants to die alone, they do. If they want to die with particular people in the room, they do. We may not be able to control whether we die, but we do control that final moment in this way.

> At the residential hospice, I was honoured to help facilitate reconciliation between a mother and her estranged adult daughter. They had not spoken for more than ten years and lived in different provinces when the mother received a diagnosis of stage four lung cancer. The daughter decided to visit and nurse her mother for her final weeks. She moved into the hospice room and never left her mother's side. Family brought food and meals for her. Her mother's PPS was still 40 and they had long conversations together. Her mother shared that she didn't want her daughter to be with her at the end, because she wanted her to have positive memories after so many difficult ones. One day, after six long weeks inside the hospice room, an aunt came to the hospice and suggested the daughter join her to eat together in the hospice dining room. When the daughter returned to her mother an hour later, she had died. The mother got what she wanted – dying during the only window of aloneness she'd been given.

For this reason, it is helpful to arrange a vigil schedule that allows for both time alone for the dying person, as well as time with others. Time alone allows the dying person to reflect on their life, and also to do spiritual practice. It takes the pressure off of every moment counting, and lets there be spaciousness in the room.

For the vigil, the dying person may not appear to participate much. Therefore, it will likely need to be led by someone else. If the dying person has a spiritual practice, this is the time to invite spiritual friends to visit and to spend time alone with the dying person. They may want specific prayers or chants to be said for them or with them.

Some people have chosen to prepare music playlists for the vigil. This can be favourite pop songs, songs with meaning from their life, or simply peaceful songs. Appropriate music can make it easier to be in the room and waiting for the final breath. It can ease any tension in the room and make it easier to just sit together. Waiting for the end can be one of the hardest parts of the journey.

A Buddhist will want to have time in the room for Sangha members and spiritual friends to say prayers and chants. The most common chants include mantras involving Amithaba (boundless space) and Amitayus (boundless time). They will also want spiritual friends to encourage spiritual aspirations. Even as the mind fades from this lifetime, they will appreciate encouragement to be calm and fearless as they enter the formless state of rebirth.

People with other spiritual practices will also benefit from having support from spiritual teachers and friends. It can be easy to forget aspirations made in other periods of one's life and caregivers and spiritual friends are helpful when they give gentle reminders. Of course, it is important not to pressure the dying person to do anything they no longer want to do, even if they had previously expressed an interest in it. Priorities change at end of life, and often simply breathing with good awareness in the moment becomes the most important imperative, as other priorities simply drop away.

Final minutes

For the final moments of life, all that is needed is loving kindness and patience. Calmness and peaceful conversations help benefit everyone in the room. Time does funny things in the final moments, and it's easy to want to rush past these final moments and get on to the many tasks that await, like planning for the memorial service or notifying other family members and friends. But really, all that is needed in the final moment is a willingness to just sit and be present for one of life's greatest mysteries. There are not many such opportunities for most of us.

> Irfan was a family man, through and through. His wife had been diagnosed with Parkinson's Disease ten years earlier. He had kept her home with him for as long as possible by hiring several PSWs to assist with all her care. He loved her dearly. On the final morning of her life, he arrived early at the hospice on Sunday morning as he always did. He sat quietly with his wife of 62 years. He touched the

Host to her lips and told her he loved her for the millionth time. And she took her last breath. According to Irfan, it could not have been scripted any better if he'd tried.

You may want to lightly touch your loved one for one last time. Not intrusively, but just to connect. You will likely have a laser focus on the breathing which tells you everything you want to know. At this stage, the breathing might be so faint, that you cannot hear anything. Listening for in-breaths that will be so quiet, and you only know it's still happening by watching the chest move slightly. Many people miss the final moment because it's so quiet and peaceful. Like an old clock that slowly winds down until there is no more movement. One moment the body is still taking tiny sips of air and the next moment there's an exhalation and no more in-breath.

Regardless of your specific spiritual practice, you will want to ensure that the space around the dying person is calm and peaceful. If there are family conflicts, this is not the time to address them. The dying person needs nothing greater than an emotionally open space.

You may have heard that dying people need *permission* to die. Much has been written about families giving permission to their loved ones to leave them. My experience tells me that the dying person is looking after their own needs as they approach death. They don't need anyone's permission to do anything. What does seem to help, though, is to be *reassured* by their loved ones that they will be okay once the dying person is gone. Permission implies that the loved ones are in charge of death, and I believe this is a wrong starting point. The dying person is living their own life, and letting go of a good lifetime can be hard, so encouragement and reassurance can be helpful.

> My mother-in-law was the matriarch of the family. She loved her five children and all the many grandchildren, and had devoted much of her retirement years to spending time with them all. As she neared the end of a long cancer journey, she spoke openly of her worry about how everyone would get along without her. She admitted that if she didn't worry about her family, she wouldn't know herself! She seemed to be hanging on to something, even though she'd stopped eating and drinking. Her children took the time to reassure her that they would be okay without her, and promised to hear her voice when they thought about making good food choices. With that, she was able to let go and she died peacefully after saying goodbye to all of them.

Some families like to sit together and reminisce during the Vigil. They share stories about the entire dying person's life. They conjure up the whole experience of life, and help themselves remember more than just the recent disease and suffering.

This remembering of the life is not for the dying person clinging to this lifetime, but rather a way for the people remaining to honour the life. It is a helpful part of the grieving process to be fully present and fully appreciative.

Sometimes the final moment doesn't go as planned. Maybe the dying person wants one thing and the family members want another thing. It's important to keep flexibility in your wishes for how it will go. Just because you missed the dying moment does not mean that the dying person loved you any less. It is not helpful to attach too much meaning to the final scripting. In fact, it is common for dying people to die without the spouse or partner in the room, or whoever might be considered "the closest one." Knowing this might lesson the guilt that arises if you are not in the room for the actual last breath.

> One of my first community hospice patients completely missed his wife's death moment. His wife was dying of Stage 4 Pancreatic Cancer. One morning she woke up and insisted that he needed to get the winter tires put on the car in case she needed to be driven to hospital later. Dutifully, he completed the task only to learn that she'd died ten minutes after he left the house. She was with their son and wasn't alone, but he was furious. He thought this meant she didn't love him. He had to struggle with this for a while before he could accept that he'd done what she wanted, and her death had happened as she wanted.

First moments after death

When the body breathes its last breath, notice the inclination to move. Resist it. Slow down. Just sit. Everything can wait. A bit. It might feel like there is much to do, but it can all wait. NO RUSH!!! The most useful advice I can give to caregivers is to resist the urgency to kick into motion after the last breath. It's okay to make a few calls or send notifications to a few people at the top of the notification chart, but even those can wait. Death is a mystery, and most people don't have many opportunities to witness it. So lean into the experience! Be fearless about staying present, even when you want to run and hide.

Observe the body. Notice what happens to the body in the transition between life and death. Watch carefully and see if you can notice when consciousness (or spirit or soul, or whatever you call that living part) exits. What do you see? What do you feel? How does it affect the people in the room?

Only after everyone has breathed deeply and is ready to move, do you need to think about the next step. Someone will need to *pronounce the death* eventually. If you are in a hospital or residential hospice, you can notify a nurse who will enter the room, listen for a heartbeat, and make the determination. Hospital beds are frequently in high demand, and families may find they are urged to say goodbye to the body within a few hours. Residential hospices are usually a bit more flexible since it takes more time to get a person ready to move to the hospice, and they will often allow up to 24 hours in the room.

If you are at home, don't call 911. If there is a life-limiting illness, you probably have an EDITH order in place. An EDITH order is an Expect Death in the Home document that a doctor has filled out previously stating that the person has a disease that is progressing toward death. The forms differ slightly by province, but are generally accepted throughout Canada.[50] An EDITH order is similar to a POLST in the United States. In these cases, death at home does not require a coroner to visit. It's as simple as calling the palliative care doctor or nurse and making the report. They will visit and pronounce the death, but not in an urgent manner.

There are many laws related to death, but in most jurisdictions, there is no rush when death is not sudden and has been planned for. There is no law in Ontario for how quickly a body must be removed from a home after the body has died of a life-limiting illness. There are practical concerns related to time of year, and how quickly the body might start to decompose. Cooler temperatures slow the process down, and ice packs or dry ice can help extend this time. The first sign of decomposition is noticed in the smells that the body produces as it begins to break down. Keeping a body without special cooling considerations for up to two days is not usually an issue in most parts of Canada in most seasons.

> My friend accompanied his wife to the end of her life. She was able to stay at home for her final weeks because he could manage her care with the support of the community palliative team. They were lucky that she didn't have severe or difficult pain or medical needs, and her final days were peaceful and calm. Knowing death was coming allowed them to plan and prepare for what they wanted to happen after her death. When she died, there was no rush to move her, and the family could gather around her for prayers. He washed her body one final time and placed her in a casket, hand-made by a carpenter friend. A room in the house had been prepared in advance to accommodate the casket and be a peaceful place for the family to spend time grieving. As this happened during the pandemic, there was no expectation of having a visitation for friends, though in an earlier plan he had hoped people could visit in small numbers. He had planned to use ice under the casket, but instead simply cooled the room and then moved the casket outside for some of the time, relying simply on the chill of winter. The body was at home for the three days until the Funeral Mass, and from there was transported to a cemetery out of the

---

50 EDITH forms, Ontario version: palliativecare.ca
EDITH forms, British Columbia version: gov.bc.ca

city that allows for burials with caskets that decompose easily. With the help of a few friends and an accommodating funeral service company, this ending honoured her life, and allowed my friend to show love and care all the way to the end. He appreciated being on his own time schedule, and it softened the shift from caregiving to mourning.

Good organizational skills and pre-planning make this time after death less stressful. This is not the time to begin thinking about or planning the memorial service. Hopefully those major decisions have already been made, and one simple call can put them into motion. Also, a ready contact list and phone tree can be useful to activate in a simple way. Written announcements are helpful to prepare in advance, with a plan for who will do what.

Planning for death notification probably involves some thought around use of social media. Decide in advance whose social media to use. Make sure that passwords are known if the dying person wants their social media used for this purpose. Some social media platforms expect to be notified when the person has died, and to either delete the profile or transfer it to a profile to be listed as a deceased person.

As more and more Canadians move to do cremations rather than burials, it is becoming common to have visitations right where the body died during the first 24 hours. No need to pay for expensive visitations at funeral homes, but instead invite close friends and family members to attend for final farewells. It is kind to allow individuals to have private time with the deceased person to say personal goodbyes, in addition to having large gatherings.

Teens typically have a greater squeamishness than kids to a dead body. At the residential hospice, a mother of a 16-year-old girl died of ovarian cancer. Her daughter had visited regularly during the final weeks, but her mother had died during the night. The following morning the teen came back to the hospice, and I passed her standing in the hall outside the door. She admitted she was too scared to go into the room to see the body alone. I offered to accompany her, and she agreed. I opened the door and she peered in from the hallway. Eventually she walked in, stood behind me, and grabbed my hand in silence. We stood there together for a few moments until she was ready to leave. She wrote a card to me thanking me for helping her do what she knew her future self would be glad she had done, but which she couldn't have done alone.

There are many reasons to let a dying body rest in the same position as their last breath. Buddhists believe that this allows for the death Bardo to occur without disturbance. Ideally, a body is left untouched for up to 72 hours, during which time a trained practitioner can notice when consciousness has departed fully. The death Bardo is the stage when planning for the next lifetime occurs when consciousness reviews the karma of one's most recent lifetime. The death Bardo explanation might be similar to the reckoning that Christians believe happens as they enter the Pearly Gates of heaven, but without the specific timeframes that Buddhism recommends. During this time, the crown chakra at the top of one's head is never touched, not even during a final cleaning, because this is believed to be the place that consciousness enters and ultimately exits the body for good.

Buddhists believe that consciousness leaves the body for most unawakened beings (which is most of us) within the first 24 hours. Practically speaking, they also acknowledge that it is difficult to leave the body undisturbed for the full 72 hours in modern society. Life simply moves too fast now and we no longer have this as an option, as hospitals and residential hospices make room for more dying people.

Interestingly, many of the desert religions like Judaism and Islam believe in moving quickly after the final breath to have the body buried within 24 hours. These guidelines relate back to the time before modern death rituals when this was necessary to prevent infections and strong decay in high temperatures, but the practices continue today. They are followed by longer mourning periods like sitting shiva that allow for the community to come together to grieve more fully.

❦

Humans are natural storytellers, and the story of the death is one that will be repeated many times. Listen carefully to the story that emerges naturally, and make sure it is one you can live with. Maybe tell the story together so there's some semblance of unity to a family version. If you or some of the others have missing parts, make sure you all share the same information, as this helps with the collective grieving process. Try to settle on a version that brings peace and understanding to all, and doesn't perpetuate traumatic or troublesome views. Recognize that the grieving process unfolds better with complete stories and not guilt-inducing versions.

> Despite being with hundreds of dying people and their families in their final days, I have only been in the room with two people as they took their last breath. One of these times I was listening to a daughter tell the story of how her mother escaped from Nazi soldiers not once but twice as a 12-year-old girl in Poland. The story was compelling and the daughter was crying with such pride and joy to be this woman's daughter. At one moment, we realized that her mother had died during the story telling without either of us noticing, even though

we'd been holding her hand and huddled around her. She became distressed and felt guilty for missing the moment. Upon reflection, she was so grateful that after a lifetime of struggle, her mother had simply had the most peaceful death possible. When her sister arrived, she told the story of how peaceful the death had been, and had totally moved beyond her guilt of missing the moment.

Final Wash of Body

If dying can be messy, death is even messier. Therefore, most bodies need a gentle wash to remove the evidence of this final release. Bodies release urine, excrement, and often secretions from all body orifices. This might sound gross, but really, it's just an external verification of the release that happens at the level of consciousness. It's also common to perform limited body care in the final days, as the care can be so painful and stressful to the dying person. They might not have had a sponge bath recently, so they will have normal sweat and odour. Culturally, we might be programmed to think of this as disgusting, but it is a normal response of death.

In hospital or residential hospice, staff will perform the washing duties. This often happens within minutes or hours after the last breath, and takes only a short time. Rigor mortis sets in within two to four hours, making it more difficult later, and this lasts for several days before relaxing a bit again. Rigor mortis is when the body limbs stiffen at death due to chemical changes in the muscles. This task of washing the body a final time is considered an auspicious act that goes beyond simply cleaning, and staff typically bring a reverence for the life of the deceased to the task.

Most of us have never been offered a chance to watch how quickly a body decomposes and have literally no idea of what's normal. When I worked at the residential hospices, it was common for families to assume that the body would be too gross and disgusting to look at within a few hours of death. Staff encouraged families to take their time saying goodbye to the body for the last time, and one family took it so literally that they asked if they could leave the body with the hospice for six days while waiting for a family member to finish a work shift. (The answer to that was "sorry, but NO; that's too long".)

At home, professionals can be on-hand to perform final cleaning of the body. If not, family members or friends may want to do so. They can make it be as quick or drawn out as they want, and as perfunctory or ceremonial as they desire.

The final part is dressing the body in the clothing that they will leave this world in. It is common to cut the clothing to make it easier to dress the body, often with a slit down the back, and then tucked in carefully so it looks tidy on top. This is recommended even throughout the final 21 days, if the person is staying in bed fully. This is another example of the practicality necessary in the dying process.

Death Doulas

Some families will want to hire the services of a Death Doula to assist them with the final washing of the body, and other tasks just after the dying person takes their last breath. Ideally, a relationship with a Death Doula begins long before the death moment, so that the Death Doula has an opportunity to meet the dying person and determine their wishes as well as the wishes of the family members and friends.

The Death Doula movement is still relatively new to Canada, and is completely unregulated. Some Doulas think that lack of regulation is a good thing because it allows for the role to stay detached from the medical field. Others are advocating for greater standardization as a way of increasing the growth of this role and ensuring the public of high-quality work. This variation between Death Doulas makes it hard to speak universally about what a Death Doula actually is or does. The Death Doula field is much the same as where Birth Doulas and Midwives were 25 years ago in Canada. There is also some inconsistency in title, with some using the term Death Doula and others preferring Death Midwife (aligning with birth midwives), End of Life Doula (more than just death), or Thanatologist. A Thanatologist studies death, and programs on thanatology can be both theoretical or practical.

According to the End of Life Doula Association, "End of Life (Death) Doulas empower, educate, and encourage people and their families to be involved in making decisions."[51] Their education covers topics such as caring for the dying, caring for the family, caring for a loved one, self-care, grief, bereavement, and advocacy. Their services typically include counselling sessions, forgiveness rituals, and at-home funerals, as well as many other services for families that typically fall between the gaps.

One of the ways to describe what a Death Doula does is to share this poem by Judith McGill, a Death Doula and founder of Community Deathcare Canada,[52] a website that organizes and promotes deathcare services across the country. For a listing of Death Doulas across Canada, as well as other professionals working as experts in death dying, consult the Community Deathcare website. Judith also provides direct services to families and loved ones through the Dragonfly Collective.[53]

Deep Abiding Love
After death, those of us that are left behind, bear the task of helping the person, our beloved on the other side, know their worth and continue to be awake and filled with consciousness in the spirit world.

---

51 End of Life Doula Association. endoflifedoulaassociation.org

52 Community Deathcare Canada. communitydeathcare.ca

53 Dragonfly Collective. dragonflycollective.ca

We do this by silencing ourselves, finding inner stillness and inwardly remembering our loved one, his way in the world, his gesture in the world – a particular aspect of his movement, stance, facial expression or a phrase that makes it easier for us to draw near him through our love of him.

This re-membering him will make it more possible to hold him close to our heart and then reflect on his soul's purpose by what he brought to the world through his deeds and actions.

We work at re-membering how he used his gifts and talents to bring love and beauty into the world, to re-member his substance and how he met life's obstacles, what he had the grace to overcome and what he gained through this overcoming. To hold even those aspects of his soul that were yet unyielding and untamed so that we are able to place the whole person before us with love and mercy, acknowledging his soul's journey.

In this way, we support the life review he is taken up with at this time and assist him to find a certain peace with the process of returning back to the beginning, the unity.

And in this way, our relationship transforms, and the dialogue begins where out of our deep and abiding love, our loved one inspires us to continue striving on our own unique path. Forever changed by his example.

When we want to be connected to our loved one, we remember to have faith that he will continue to guide our will and loving intention so that we may bring loving, merciful acts into the world.

Until we are united again, we go forward honouring who he was in the world so that his soul's purpose and deeds may live in the world through us.

Judith McGill, Death Midwife
and founder of Dragonfly Collective

Death Doula services are not currently covered by any provincial health plan. This means Death Doulas need to be entrepreneurial and establish a self-employment private practice to make a viable business for themselves. They also need to continue to advocate for this new role and help convince Canadians of their value. Some Death Doulas are drawn to the role as a calling and simply perform it informally as an unpaid Volunteer, and this is another option.

The role of Death Doula overlaps significantly with the role of Hospice Palliative Care Social Worker, which is also not universally well-funded or respected. Both share a focus on the needs of both the dying person and their loved ones, and the communication and wishes between them. One distinction between these two roles might be said to be that Death Doulas tend to focus more on needs related to the body and Social Workers tend to focus more on interpersonal psychosocial relations, but these are generalizations, and they overlap more than not.

Death Doulas are generally spiritualists, who do believe in a more spiritual experiencing of death at end of life. Their clients are typically people who consider themselves spiritual, but do not adhere to established religious traditions. As they approach their end of life, they don't have a community to rely on to guide them through the final passage.

There are only a few training programs for Death Doulas in Canada. The End of Life Doula Association of Canada recommends these two programs: The Institute of Traditional Medicine – Contemplative End of Life Care Program, a popular option for weekends-only in Toronto, Ontario,[54] or Douglas College – End of Life Doula Program, a single 32-hour course based in New Westminster, British Columbia[55]. There are also individuals leading their own education programs. Cassandra Yonder offers some Death Midwifery education services from Cape Breton, Nova Scotia,[56] and administers the very popular Death Midwifery in Canada FaceBook group. Sarah Kerr provides many online Death Doula trainings from Calgary, Alberta, that are available to anyone with an internet connection.[57] For those interested in Thanatology, there is a Death Education program at Kings College in the University of Western in London, Ontario, that offers degrees and certifications in thanatology.[58]

It's easy to get overwhelmed by all the various needs at end of life of the dying person and all the various people affected. If anyone is feeling like needs are not being met adequately with traditional roles, hiring a Death Doula may help fill those gaps. Death Doulas like Ruth MacKay and Sarah Farr help dying people and their families feel well supported, and offer compassionate and consistent voices throughout illnesses and dying journeys.[59] Their services are often offered *à la carte*, where you can choose exactly what you need. They are easily personalized, and often bring in rituals and connection to the sacred that bring greater meaning to the experience.

> We know that so many individuals and families feel lost as they grapple with life transitions and come face to face with the reality of aging, dying, death and grief. We live in the biggest city in Canada, with a myriad of programs and services, but so often they can be confusing, disconnected, under-resourced and ultimately impersonal.

54 Institute of Traditional Medicine (2021). *Contemplative End of Life Care Program.* itmworld.org

55 Douglas College. *End of Life Doula Program.* douglascollege.ca

56 Beyond Yonder (2014). *Death Midwifery Education.* deathmidwifery.ca/death_education.html

57 Soul Passages (2021). *Death Doula Education.* soulpassages.ca/programs

58 Kings College at University of Western Ontario. *Thanatology degrees and certificates.* kings.uwo.ca

59 MacKay, R. and Farr, S. *Death Doulas.* wishstone.ca

In much of our Canadian society, we no longer know how to be with a dying person. As End-of-Life Doulas, we provide a consistent and supportive presence throughout the journey, bringing compassion and warmth alongside knowledge and experience.

At Wishstone we know that "All that matters in the end, matters now."

Ruth MacKay and Sarah Farr, Co-founders of Wishstone

Options for disposal of body

Even if one slows down after the dying moment, eventually a plan for disposing of the body will have to be implemented. And there are lots of options, with more coming all the time. Hopefully the dying person will have thought about and discussed their preference and clarified this in writing in their Advanced Care Plans (ACPs).

One of the basic questions to consider about disposal of the body that ultimately shapes many other decisions is the question of burial or cremation. Cremation rates (compared to burials) in Canada have risen from 52.4% in 2004 to 73.1% in 2019, and are predicted to continue to rise one percent per year for the foreseeable future.[60] Rising rates are attributed to an interest in lowering costs, concern for the environment, and multicultural influences that support cremations.

Funeral and Memorial Service Options

Burial options require one to use formal cemeteries for the internment of the body. Bodies must be placed into designated caskets for burial, and cemetery plots must be cared for and paid for in advance. In most jurisdictions across Canada, it is illegal to bury a body on private land.

In some cultures, it is common to visit cemeteries, either weekly or on anniversaries. More recently, people are finding other ways to remember loved ones and are using more on-line options for creating genealogical records. Traditionally families bought shared plots together and the expectation was that family members would be buried together. This tradition has been challenged with more frequent divorces and some people deciding to opt out of family expectations, thereby making the exclusive family enclave less complete.

One of the other issues associated with burial is the role that funeral homes play in brokering the relationship with the cemetery. Funeral homes today are no longer small, privately-owned businesses, and since 2015, larger funeral homes in Canada are buying out family funeral homes at outrageous rates. Park Lawn (a large funeral home owner across Canada) has even become a publicly traded stock. Funeral

---

60 cremationassociation.org

Traditional Funeral Home	• No fees on website (typically $8000-20,000) • Full service – including visitation of the body, embalming, meeting spaces, and food • Lots of upselling to grieving families • Allow family to do as little as possible
Progressive Funeral Home	• Fees posted on website to see and compare • Packages of all kind from small (under $5000) to large • Work with family wishes • Lean toward containing costs
Alternative	• Crematorium handles cremation only (under $2000) • Greatest family involvement • Take ashes to meeting space in condo building, restaurant, temple/church, or home • Cheapest cost

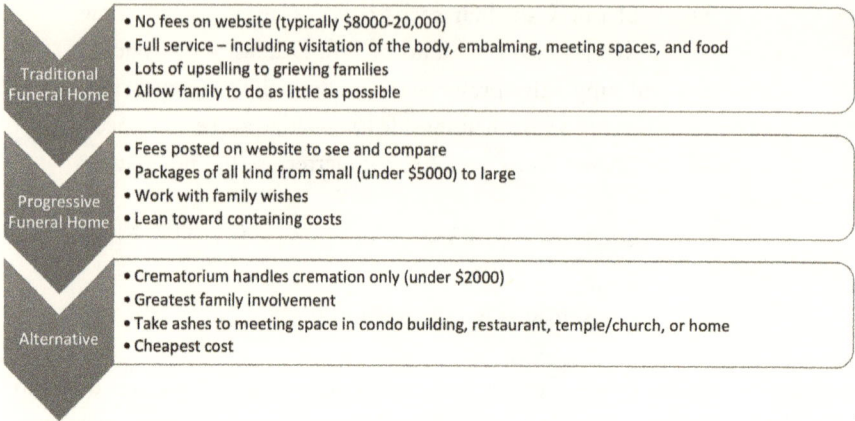

homes in the past were more local and integrated into the community, but most funeral homes today are franchised businesses that have earned the reputation of taking advantage of grieving families to link love and expense, thereby driving up the cost of the final farewell.

It is common for funerals that involve both visitation and funeral services to cost between $8,000 and $20,000, including the cost of an expensive casket. This is no judgment on families who want big funerals, but hopefully these wishes are in line with the dying person's wishes, and not just the wishes of the funeral home or guilt-stricken family members. It is useful to know that cremation profit margins are around 65 per cent while funeral services have margins of 90 per cent.[61] As they say, death is big business!

In response to the accusation of "grief bullying", a new wave of progressive funeral homes has opened up. These funeral homes are often small, yet still offer a range of services, and they openly discuss cost and are more respectful of family choices. They show prices on their website for their packages, and allow for containment of costs offering complete packages for $5,000 or $6,000. These include more environmentally friendly options for caskets, including casket rentals. They often have words like "simple" or "alternative" in their names.

Cremation is the process of applying high heat to a body to complete the decomposition in a matter of hours. Cremation occurs in a crematorium, sometimes a standalone business and sometimes attached to a funeral home. It is not necessary to go through the services of a funeral home if all you want is a cremation service. Crematoriums will arrange for pickup of the body through a 24/7 transport service, and will notify you a few days later when the ashes are ready for pick up. Cremation services can cost less than $2000, without a memorial service.

Cremation is becoming more and more popular in Canada. As our population increases, cemetery spaces get ever more crowded and more expensive. While tra-

---

61 Taylor, F. ((March 23, 2015). *Funeral Income Stocks Offers Both Income and Growth.* theglobeandmail.com

ditional Muslim and Judeo-Christian religions still often teach burial practices, they are based on previous cultures that had ready burial lands. They also came from countries of warm climates where temperatures were often high, requiring the quick need to dispose of a body into the ground to prevent decomposition. These issues are less relevant today. Asia has traditionally preferred cremation to burial, and continues to do so. In Canada, as recent immigration trends come increasingly from Asia, and fewer Canadians practice religious beliefs that support burials, the number of cremations in Canada continues to grow.

Cremation is a lot more convenient than burial. Ashes can be taken to any site and a memorial service can be done anywhere at any time. There are no rules around where memorial services can and cannot be held. Laws regarding cremation ashes only differ slightly across Canada, but it is important to check locally before making any plans. Laws in Ontario currently limit where ashes can be buried – only in formal cemeteries. However, ashes can be distributed in partial amounts in almost any public or private property in Ontario. More and more dying people are designating where they want their ashes sprinkled, often in places that had meaning for them in life.

> A few years back, we held a meaningful ritual with the ashes of my mother and father, who had both died a number of years before. At an annual Cottage Weekend, my siblings and our cousins went to a favourite fishing spot of the long-deceased parent of the cousins. Years before, the cousins had paid a visit here with their parents' ashes. They ceremoniously sprinkled some of the remains at the old fishing site. We told stories and laughed and remembered these special people. And now we eight cousins know that our four parents are "together".   *David Clark, brother-in-law*

Green Burials, or environmentally friendly burials, are still a relatively new idea for Canadians. The Green Burial Canada website lists ten sites nationally, from British Columbia to Nova Scotia. In Ontario, in 2021, there are still only two cemeteries that meet their criteria.[62] In these cemeteries, bodies are placed in shrouds, wicker baskets, or cardboard boxes that quickly decompose. There is no individual nameplate, but a group nameplate to the side of the burial site. The site gets reused and there are trees and grass growing around. This option is considered more environmentally friendly than even regular cremation, but locations tend not to be close to urban centres and may not always be convenient, especially if you want to visit regularly.

Costs for green burials tend to be cheaper than traditional cemeteries because the individual person's land use is smaller and the ongoing maintenance fees are shared with a larger number of families, but cost is not usually the driver of this option. Families interested in choices with a lower environmental impact usually

---

62 Green Burials Canada. *Approved Cemeteries.* greenburialcanada.ca

choose to not embalm the body and use a biodegradable (or more easily degradable) casket. More information on Green Burials can be found on the website for Green Burials Canada, and they even have volunteers trained to meet with you and discuss the options with you.[63]

There are more options coming for body disposal besides cremation and burial, as entrepreneurs experiment with ways to break down the body. One newer option is the mushroom suit: a suit embedded with mushroom spores explicitly chosen to break down the body faster.[64] This option could work in a green burial cemetery, and the idea works along the lines of compost accelerators.

Another option that started as a scene in the TV series "Breaking Bad" is the use of hydrofluoric acid to produce caustic burns that destroy body tissue. There is a company in Ottawa that is researching this option.[65] Unlike the TV scene where the bathtub where the body is being destroyed dissolves and destroys the house instead of simply destroying the body, a proper container to hold the solution is the key to success.

Cremation is usually thought of as using high heat, but alkaline hydrolases is a newer form that uses other methods.[66] Instead, it combines water, alkaline chemicals, heat, and sometimes pressure and agitation to accelerate natural decomposition. This decomposition process is the same as what happens during burial, but the process is accelerated. It releases water without any remaining DNA in it at the end, and uses relatively little energy or time, making it better for the environment than cremation.

Crematoria, in general, are also getting greener, and those that use lower temperature ovens are also being researched. As more people are seeking out greener options for disposal of the body, one option might be fires that require lower heat than standard cremation ovens and therefore lower energy footprints. This option also avoids the problem that comes with the burning of mercury fillings from dental work at high temperatures and releasing these fumes into the environment.

Different crematoria have different rates of emissions. Since 2014, the Mount Pleasant Cemetery in Toronto has one of the lowest rates of emissions in North America. They purchased large burners and a filtration system that utilizes air circulation to fuel the cremation. This means that mercury from teeth does not get released into the environment. Clearly there are cleaner ways to complete the cremation process, and it is worth asking a few questions before you choose a crematorium if these issues are important to you.

---

63 Ibid.

64 'Mushroom Death Suit'. (April 15, 2014). huffpost.com

65 Helmenstine, A.M. (June 30, 2019). *Dissolving a Body in Hydrofluoric Acid, as on "Breaking Bad"*. thoughtco.com

66 Cremation Association of North America. *Alkaline Hydrolysis*. cremationassociation.org

I have had many conversations with family members about the pros and cons of burial and cremation. However, one discussion stands out to me. I was meeting with a grandson in Ontario whose grandmother was dying. She had spent most of her life in the United States, and had pre-paid a funeral plot in New York. He was wondering whether he could afford a burial, as she originally wanted. He was afraid to Google search the cost of transporting a body across the American border on his work computer and asked for my assistance. Together (and on MY work computer) we discovered the cost was more than he could afford, as borders require a declaration and special taxes. Fortunately, he spoke with his grandmother before she died, and together they agreed to do a cremation in Canada and a memorial service in the United States.

Buddhism comes from Asia, and the custom is to follow the local culture of preferring cremation over burial. Cremation in India often occurs outside on large burning Ghats on the edges of rivers. The most well-known and touristed sites are the Ghats of Varanasi on the banks of the Ganges River. I visited this site twice and both times was struck by the calmness and serenity of the local Indians as they set up large bonfires of timber logs, chatting casually with each other as they placed bodies on top of these pyres and lit them. People roamed around freely with no ropes or cordoned off areas in sight. The smell of burning flesh and hair was putrid, the air was smoky and it was difficult to breathe, but the mood was light and almost friendly.

Cremation produces a fine ash with pieces of bone, and they often leave large pieces of bone with cremations in Asia. These bone remnants, combined with hairs and relics, are saved from great Buddhist teachers and placed into statues and buildings to preserve and honour them forever. Relics known as *sariras* are tiny white balls that are distinguishable within the remains of awakened beings, and are thought to be the physical manifestation of the awakened mind. It is possible they are created by changes to the endocrine system as the being awakens, including hardening of the pineal glands. It is believed that these relics can move about on their own, and do not necessarily follow rules of gravity or place. This is another example of the open time and space portals around death, if you choose to believe these tales.

Whether you believe in the magical properties of relics or not, they are a cultural part of Buddhism in Asia, and they support the practice of cremation for awakened beings, as the cremation process is necessary to remove the relics from the body. Relics can be visually seen by anyone and are suggestive of the mystery of death that I continue to be fascinated by.

However, for unawakened beings, Buddhists are more open to body disposal options, and can accept both burial and cremation options for their practitioners.

It would be difficult to understand how a large and expensive funeral is not creating attachment to the body or this lifetime, and practically speaking Buddhism has less to say about how to dispose of the body, and more about doing what's necessary to dispose of the body and moving on.

Some people find discussion about body disposal to be gross and disgusting. Others find it irrelevant. And still others find they have very strong opinions about it. Regardless where one lands regarding choices, a decision must be made about what to actually do with the body once the breathing stops and life has ended. Ideally, this decision has been made long before, and a simple phone call activates it all.

6

Spirituality

Equanimity

Regardless of the process chosen to dispose of the body, a spiritual practitioner will want to exercise equanimity toward death. That is, to remember they have always known that life was impermanent. It's fascinating how the ego resists remembering this. We know this from birth, yet we seem to play games with this knowledge. So many times, I hear people say something about "...*if* I die...". I gently correct them to say, "you mean *when* you die...". It reminds me of the intensity of the human wiring. The human form is tied to believing that only this lifetime matters, and the successes and relationships of this lifetime are what counts. The attachment to form, with the body being its strongest representative, is the strongest attachment of all.

Some people are able to use love to miraculously overcome this wiring of being tied to the human form, and find compassion in the face of death. Several years ago, at the Symposium for Contemplative Care at the Garrison Institute, I was honoured to share a meal with Frank Ostaseski. Over a delicious vegetarian meal, he shared stories of the people he had met along the way as he sat with hundreds of dying people. He remembers them all, and the impact they had on him. I reckon that he has the greatest humility I have ever come face to face with, and this comes with his experience of sitting with death so closely and frequently. Frank is a co-founder of the San Francisco Zen Hospice, established in 1987 to deal with the tragedy of AIDS. He knows death up close, and continues to lean into death, and not away from its intensity. He recently published a book of the lessons he learned from death that are as deep as they are simple:

Frank Ostaseski's Five Invitations[67]

1. Don't wait.
2. Welcome everything, push away nothing.

---

67 Ostaseski, F. (March 14, 2017). *The Five Invitations: Discovering What Death Can Teach Us About Living Fully.*

3. Bring your whole self to the experience.
4. Find a place of rest in the middle of things.
5. Cultivate "don't know mind."

It's ironic that one has to die, or be close to dying, before one is eligible for spiritual support in our Canadian healthcare system. Illness during life is viewed through the lens of physical pain. Doctors and nurses work hard to provide treatment for physical pain to take you back to living. If the physical pain is really bad, one might get emotional support by adding social work services. Sadly, more and more social work services in the medical system are pointed toward getting people out of hospital in the form of discharge planning, and not addressing emotional or psychological pain. And then only as one gets close to dying, and only if one's situation is bad enough to land them in hospital, does one also get spiritual support. There are few spiritual supports going into homes to address spiritual pain.

For people preparing to work as chaplains, there are a few options for places to work. Primary options are in hospitals and prisons. A smaller number of chaplains work in Long Term Care Homes or Residential Hospices. Their work often overlaps with that of social workers, in that they are asked to provide both spiritual and emotional support. They also provide support both before the death and after the death to grieving families. They are commonly called when families seem overwhelmed and medical staff do not know how to handle the emotions.

Immigrants from Europe brought their own religions and spirituality with them when they settled In Canada, and have often tried to impose their beliefs over indigenous spiritual beliefs. Respect for others' beliefs has never been a universal principle in this country, and we are slow to observe this properly even to this day. We might have religious freedom enshrined in The Charter of Human Rights and Freedoms, but on a daily basis we overstep others' spiritual beliefs with great impunity. The reason for this is that it is hard to recognize the validity of others' faiths. The mind naturally believes the right of the ego to its own superiority. We can more easily move beyond the judgmental mind by at least starting with spirituality as a human right, and attempting to remain open and accepting to others' spiritual views.

It's not okay to impose our spirituality on anyone else. Whether we possess the dominant religious belief of a given group, or a minority view, we owe it to everyone to show up with a curious mind and an open heart. We are called to honour the spiritual choices of everyone. Whether one has the title of multifaith explicitly labeled in the role of chaplain, it is highly prized in the role of chaplain. This is not necessarily historical, when Christian chaplains dominated the role, but rather reflects the actual make-up of Canada today.

That said, there are many different ways to support people spiritually at end of life. For many people, spiritual support shows up in the form of a conversation. A conversation with a chaplain distinguishes itself from regular chatty conversation about the mundane world by the fearlessness of the chaplain to discuss anything. Anything might mean truly anything!

Religion is an organized way to explain the meaning of life and death. It offers a narrative overview and framework to make sense of things that don't easily make sense – like where did we come from and where are we going. It also explains why things are like they are.

At end of life, a dying person often needs help putting words to the rumblings in their head. The kinds of questions that occupy the mind of the dying person are not the kind that occupy the mind of a healthy and living person. There may be no history of talking about these questions with families and friends, and it may feel safer to discuss these questions with someone who is inherently neutral and non-judgmental. A chaplain enters these conversations with no fixed agenda. There is no pre-set series of questions that a dying person must make sense of before they die. The open-ended nature of these spiritual ponderings is what some people might find unsettling, which is why the role of chaplain is such a special calling.

A multifaith chaplain working in multicultural Canada must be available to support people of all faiths with prayers and rituals. A willingness to participate in unfamiliar traditions is required to be of good service. Familiarity with the most common prayers of the major religions will go far. Most prayers have a common theme of asking forgiveness and seeking comfort. It is also useful to learn about how the various religions view the body as it is dying, to understand the context of the many rituals.

End of Life Chaplain

Chaplains work in many parts of the healthcare system, most commonly at end of life, both around the dying process and the grief stage. The Canadian Association for Spiritual Care (CASC) regulates chaplains throughout Canada. It provides "a national multi-faith organization, committed to the professional education, certification and support of people involved in spiritual care, psycho-spiritual therapy, education and research. We provide educational programs for interested persons who are preparing to become professional providers of spiritual care and psycho-spiritual therapy in a variety of institutional and community settings such as health care, corrections, education and private practice."[68]

When I decided overnight to move into hospice palliative care, I considered becoming a chaplain. In typical style, I chose the road less travelled, and not one for the intrepid! I had heard of the Foundations in Contemplative Care program based in New York City through the New York Zen Centre for Contemplative Care[69]

---

68 Canadian Association for Spiritual Care. spiritualcare.ca

69 New York Zen Centre for Contemplative Care. zencare.org

and I decided to make this the start of my training. Their nine-month program is considered to be a pre-chaplaincy program, and many graduates go on to become chaplains. Classes consisted of monthly two-day sessions in New York City, in addition to monthly video sessions with mentors and fellow students. The reading list was 22 books long, and all were new to me. Because I had been recently laid off from work and had limited finances, I made the trek each month from Toronto to New York by overnight MegaBus and stayed in a hostel that was walking distance from the Zen Centre. The transportation arrangement added to the intensity of the learning experience for me, and provided me with extensive reflection periods both before and after the trainings.

This Foundations program ended up being a fabulous training for me. It was personal, challenging, and took me into places about death I had never explored or considered. The program was only four years old at the time, and was led by two Zen monks, Sensei Chodo Campbell and Sensei Koshin Paley Ellison. As a cohort of 35 students, we looked at death up close. We planned our own funerals. We wrote death poems in the Japanese tradition. We imagined the "Dissolution of the Body". We meditated and chanted together about not squandering our precious lives. We volunteered in local hospices and palliative care units and learned to be caregivers. We learned to hold space for dying and death, in ourselves and others.

There was so much profound teaching by these monks in being with dying and death. The principles written about in Sensei Koshin's recent book, *Wholehearted: Slow Down, Help Out, Wake Up,*[70] were explored fully with the group. Together they taught us to "pay attention, be of service, and be with others."

Nine months later, I had several options to consider. I was drawn to the notion of Death Doula, but I realized that my Buddhist view of the body lessoned my interest in the body itself after the dying process released it from this lifetime. In Buddhism, the body is a vehicle for consciousness, and without consciousness the body is useless. This view is graphically represented in the Tibetan Sky Burial Ceremony, a tradition that had Vajrayana Buddhist monks assigned to cutting up the body at death and feeding it to hordes of vultures atop the Himalayan mountains. This was practical and efficient in ancient times but is no longer common in Tibet; nor is it legal in Canada, of course.

The Tibetan Sky Burial does show, however, the lack of interest in the body and lack of attachment one hopes to experience following death. Buddhists practice non-attachment throughout their life. A strong belief in an afterlife, multiple lifetimes, and/or interbeing with all things means there is no need to attach to this particular life. Death is but a transition from one lifetime to another, and the next lifetime will again have an opportunity for more relationships and love. As the Beatles once sang, "Life flows on within us and without us."

I seriously considered returning to school to train as spiritual chaplain. I got

---

70 Ellison, K.P. (June 18, 2019). *Wholehearted: Slow Down, Help Out, Wake Up.*

as far as enrolling in the Master of Pastoral Studies Program – Buddhist Stream at Emmanuel College at the University of Toronto. They offer a certificate providing training for spiritual care and psychotherapy as a spiritual care practitioner (chaplain) in public institutions like hospitals and prisons or as a psycho-spiritual therapist. They offer a popular stream that offers Buddhist Studies, including Mindfulness practices, and is the only such program in Canada.[71] Students graduate with a Masters in Pastoral Studies and preparation to qualify as a registered psychotherapist with the College for Registered Psychotherapists of Ontario.

Spiritual care training at the master's level qualifies graduates to work as chaplains in hospitals or hospices. These roles are usually filled by individuals willing to provide interfaith spiritual care to people with all kinds of spiritual beliefs.

I took one course on Buddhist Psychotherapy and enjoyed it immensely. I even received a full scholarship to cover my costs from the Buddhist Education Foundation of Canada. However, I realized that it would take six years to complete the program part-time, including all the Clinical Pastoral Education (CPE) units necessary to qualify with CASC, and I ultimately decided I didn't have that much time left in my career. I did appreciate my time with Emmanuel College and met several key people who opened up roles for me a few years down the road.

One such person is Chris Ng. She is an understated powerhouse who organizes and networks for the benefit of others, though largely keeping herself behind the scenes. She is passionate about Buddhist Psychotherapy, and in particular providing support at end of life in culturally and spiritually appropriate ways. At writing, she has nearly completed her Master in Pastoral Studies at Emmanuel College. She has also provided leadership in setting up the Toronto Centre for Applied Buddhism and leads fundraising efforts at the Buddhist Education Foundation of Canada in support of educational opportunities. In 2019, we worked together to set up Buddhist Contemplative Care at End of Life training programs that meet Hospice Palliative Care Ontario standards for hospice volunteers, but also add a Buddhist understanding of dying and death.[72]

> We are much more knowledgeable about the process of how we as babies are born to the world than about how we leave the world. Having more understanding about our exit could help us live our lives more wisely, making more informed decisions about our relationships with ourselves, with other people and the world around us.
>
> *Chris Ng, Qualifying Psychotherapist and*
> *Co-Director of Toronto Centre for Applied Buddhism*

---

71 Emmanuel College of Victoria University in the University of Toronto. emmanuel.utoronto.ca

72 Toronto Centre for Applied Buddhism (2021). Counselling Education. appliedbuddhism.ca/ counselling-education

My career/education trajectory had taken me almost to the point of becoming a Buddhist chaplain with social work skills, interested in working with dying people and their families. Instead, I would return to social work, as a spiritual social worker. I ultimately moved into setting up a private practice as a social worker, and will most likely retire from this role one day.

I researched the websites of other social workers in Toronto, and then decided to openly declare my interest in working with illness, dying, and death. I could not find anybody else willing to openly declare this interest and expertise. I deliberately decided to avoid calling myself a grief counsellor (even though I do offer grief counselling), because that's usually associated with work after a death. I have always felt that my personal calling is to work with death BEFORE death – when there are still lots of decisions to be made and plenty of conversations to be had.

I imagine that many social workers might believe that naming a skill set in dealing with illness, dying, and death might be considered morbid, and turn off people coming to deal with other issues. Rather, I have heard from clients that they like reading about this interest because it tells them that I am fearless as a therapist and deep enough to handle even their more profound issues. I have met other therapists who have joined me in their specialty and am hopeful there will be more in the years ahead.

Buddhist Support and Study

While there are many religions and spiritual practices around death, Tibetan Vajrayana Buddhism has laid out one of the most extensively mapped descriptions of what might happen after the last breath. There are plenty of sceptics who wonder where they get their maps. Buddhists point to what happens approaching death, and suggest that a similar thing repeats after the last breath. There are Tibetan masters who meditate on dying and death, and who practice dying and returning to consciousness again, and who have written about what happens. These practices also exist in other traditions, but are much less widely understood in the normative scope of those religions.

Tibetan Vajrayana Buddhists divide states of existence into unique states, with the gap between these states identified as six different stages. A Bardo is the gap in consciousness between these naturally occurring stages. There are three Bardos associated with living – life, meditation, dream, and three Bardos associated with death – dying, dharmata (just after death), and rebirth (becoming and taking form again). These states are not always discrete separable stages, since the thresholds between them are highly permeable and existence flows continuously between them.

The crossing over between the living and dying Bardos is somewhere around the drop from 40 to 30 in PPS, somewhere around 21 days. This number will differ by person, by disease, by culture, and so many other variables. But there is a crossing, and it can be recognized. And the recognizing makes life more precious and death easier to be ready to witness.

What Tibetan dying experts observe is that the dying process follows the release of the four elements before the last breath, and then these steps are repeated another time in the first three days after the last breath. The dying Bardo (the 4th Bardo) begins with the dropping of the water element, and the PPS drops from 40 to 30. The body begins to retract its life force by releasing the previously stored water in its extremities, especially the legs. This creates a spider-looking body with a big belly and spindly legs. Sometimes the body tries to release water so quickly that the calves are even drenched in liquid as the legs leak water out of the skin as fast as they can.

Outwardly, the dying person is no longer able to support themselves and they often fall when walking. This might precipitate a need to stay in bed and no longer walk to the washroom for self-toileting. This loss of independence is devastating to many Westerners who value independence, and who speak of unbearable loss of dignity when no longer able to walk to the toilet. For many, this is the turning point when the dying person is ready to die, and no longer interested in living and extending their life.

The next element to leave is when the water element fades into the earth element, and the dying person is no longer able to eat. As mentioned above, the stopping of eating is a necessary stage and is not reversible once the kidneys have begun to shut down.

The next element to leave is when the earth element fades into the fire element. In this stage, fevers are common, as the body burns away excess energy. It can also be experienced by its opposite, or extreme cold, especially in the extremities. The dying person may request blankets even though the weather is warm and caregivers are sweating. Essentially it is a rebalancing of energy through temperature.

And finally, the fire element fades into the air element, and all that matters is the breath. Nothing else. One breath at a time. Sometimes the breathing speeds up, and sometimes it is so slow it happens only once every 30 seconds, but breathing is all there is. Caregivers can be shocked to learn that sometimes this stage can last for up to three weeks, for no apparent reason. Everyone is ready, but the body just lives on. It is more common for the final stage of air element to last only a few days, or maybe a week, but it is possible for the body to receive no food or water at all, and still continue to breathe for up to 21 days.

After the body finally takes its last breath, this sequence repeats itself a full cycle once more. Careful observation of the body shows the stages of the cycle repeated. It is ideal if the body can be left to rest during this period. Resting undisturbed creates the circumstances for the best possible transition. This is similar to how recovery is improved post-surgery by holding the body still to allow the body to return to healthy functioning. Remaining undisturbed for the recommended 72 hours rarely happens in today's busy healthcare situation, when rooms are in high demand and persons who have died need to be moved out to make room for more patients in desperate need of service.

DEATH + DYING PROCESS				
I. Dissolution of Sense Faculties				
Sight	Hearing	Smell	Taste	Touch
II. Dissolution of the Material Elements				
Earth > Water Navel Smoke	**Water > Fire** Heart Mirages		**Fire > Air** Throat Sparks	**Air > Space** Secret centre Clear light
III. Clinical Death				
IV. Lamp Light (Emerging as the Four Lights)				
1. Light of Revelation: White Moonlight > Male Element				
2. Light of Augmentation: Red Light at Dawn > Female Element				
3. Light of Attainment: Complete Darkness				
4. Innate Light: Clear Sky				
Process reverses as consciousness enters a womb.				
Shared with permisson from Planet Dharma. www.planetdharma.com				

One thing to know about death that may help access your fearlessness around being a caregiver at end of life is knowing about the time and space openings that occur in dying and death. Rather than dreading death and the end of life as you know it, it may help to imagine that death is a portal to time and space openings. Time for us is thought to be experienced differently from the person who has died. Dying may be the ending of this reality of time and space, but it is the beginning of another.

Vajrayana Buddhism encourages the study of two archetypes that represent these openings at death. Amitabha is the archetype of boundless space and Amitayus is the archetype of boundless time. Meditation practices that work with these energies can help establish a connection with this openness. Sometimes this is experienced as an opening of boundaries between self and others, with an increase in empathy and relating to others as yourself. Other times it is experienced as a knowing that someone is in need without waiting for the phone call to tell you.

Both dying people and their caregivers get access to this portal of greater openness of time and space with awareness and training. It is possible for the dying person to hear conversations that are being said elsewhere in the house, even beyond the possibility of hearing with ears.

☸

Another thing that happens is that dying people often have conversations with people who have died before. In the final days before death, these conversations are extremely comforting to the dying person, when they are told that they are being welcomed home and the time is right to die.

It helps to have some experience with boundless time and space before death, so it's not so freaky at death. Otherwise, you might wonder whether you, or the dying person, are going crazy. You may think the dying person is delirious and needs more pain medication. Understanding that dying is a portal to "big mind" that includes others' minds as well can be quite comforting, and even exhilarating.

3 Living Bardos	3 Dying Bardos
Natural Bardo of This Life	Painful Bardo of Dying
Bardo of Meditation	Luminous Bardo of Dharmata – Death
Bardo of Dream and Sleep	Karmic Bardo of Becoming

Being fearless and open to these portals is the Buddhist Vajrayana training of the Dying Bardos. Bardos are gaps in consciousness. Every day people study these Bardos to make sense of the Living Bardos. Another way to witness these Bardos is to watch how the mind of the dying person fades back and forth between this world and the next. One minute they are responsive and even communicative, and the next they appear to be "gone". The ordinary person can identify this shift in the quality of the eyes. The eyes have a veil that seems to drop over them eliminating their humanness, making them appear vacant and missing. It may be for moments, and then they return. This "back and forthing" is universal, regardless of spiritual belief system (or no spiritual belief system), and there are various explanations for it.

Vajrayana Buddhism explains this phenomenon as consciousness in the gap of dharmata (Fifth Bardo), or the death moment, and they value it as much as they value the gaps experienced in the living gap of meditation. In fact, there are specific practices that encourage connecting with "the deathless state" in every archetype practice (like Amitabha or Amitayus), which is an effort to drop our obsession with form and the body, and to just experience mind without form. Imagining being without form is one of the unique meditational practices in Buddhism. The more one values this experience, the more easily one will stay with these states when we, or our loved ones, enter these states at end of life. When we learn to use open language and invite conversations around these experiences, we recognize how normal they are. One doesn't need to be a Buddhist to recognize these different states, but it helps to have some language that makes these phenomena seem normal and even expected.

Doug Duncan Sensei and Catherine Pawasarat Sensei, my primary Buddhist teachers for the last 25 years, gave an introductory talk in 2021, on this topic for

Emmanuel College at the University of Toronto. They describe Bardos in a way that can be easily accessed and understood, even for people with little knowledge of Buddhism or Bardos. This talk has been listened to and downloaded countless times, and can be found on the Emmanuel College FaceBook page.[73] They also created this image to describe the dying and death process visually, in particular the dissolving of the elements, which can be observed leading up to the death, and then repeated after the moment of death as well.[74]

Doug Sensei and Catherine Sensei have both invested a lot of teaching time helping students think about death and impermanence. As death approaches, there are a myriad of changes happening, and it is easy at this time for the mind to truly experience this impermanence.

> The best way to have a peaceful death is to prepare well in advance. In Buddhism, we are constantly recalling death as a method for helping us prepare for its eventuality. This ultimately helps us live well. Since we could die at any moment, how do we want to be now? Many of the Vajrayana Buddhist practices simulate either the Dying Bardo, or the Dharmata Bardo after death. This is particularly true of archetype or visualization practices, and even if we don't consciously know what we're doing with these rituals, they involve the rehearsing of death at a deeper level.
>
> *Catherine Pawasarat Sensei,*
> *Vajrayana Buddhist Dharma Teacher*

Doug Sensei describes the dying process as it relates to the ego. He describes the ego as the part of the self that thinks it is independent and separate from others. Much suffering is caused in the world by believing in this separateness, and acting as if death is an end, and not just a transition of consciousness. Not all people believe in rebirth into another form or another self, but doing so certainly changes the way one experiences death.

> The difficulty for most people is not understanding that the ego is, was, and always will be alone. Our connection to life and how we interact with other beings is the container in which the ego shows up and participates. In this way, preparing to die is not a task of the ego. The ego has a misappropriation error thinking that death is the end. While death is a physical end, consciousness continues on. The study

---

73 Duncan, D. and Pawasarat, C. (February 6, 2021). *Vajrayana Buddhism and the Life, Death, and Rebirth Bardos.* fb.watch/3wbu0MZz04

74 Duncan, D. and Pawasarat, C. *What Happens to Consciousness during the Death Process?* planetdharma.com

of the Bardos is studying what consciousness does when it drops the body and picks up another. Preparing for a good death would be first understanding this view of the ego, and second, living as wholesome a life as possible. One of the easiest Bardo practices is watching water turn into ice and then back into water. This shows us how natural it is for something to keep its essence, yet change its state.

Doug Duncan Sensei,
Vajrayana Buddhist Dharma Teacher

Open Portals

Death (as if it were a person) often seems to have a sense of humour, and even if we try to be closed off to open portals of time and space, we see things that otherwise have no explanation. I share this wisdom by stories, because statements about paranormal experiences on their own might seem totally unreal and unbelievable.

In final days (never weeks, just days), dying people often receive "visits" from loved ones who have died telling them their time is soon. Sometimes they see loved ones, and sometimes they just hear them, like in a dream. Maybe they have visited before and told them that the time is not right yet. But when it's only days to live, the message is always clear – We're ready for you. The time to come is now.

> A woman in her 70s had had three different cancer diagnoses. Each time, at the worst stage in the cancer, she had had a visit from her mother. Each time her mother came to tell her that the time was not yet right. She told her to keep living. When this woman had a 4th diagnosis, no one visited. Then finally, three days before her actual death, her mom visited and told her they were ready. She became unresponsive a few hours after the visit and died peacefully three days later.

Dying people can hear conversations when they are not in the same room. Even people who are hard of hearing can access a different way of hearing things at the end that does not appear to go through the ears.

> A woman in her 60s came into the residential hospice, with three adult children supporting her care. She had been "battling cancer" for two decades. Although she had agreed to come to hospice, no one in the family had spoken about the possibility of death. She still had not updated her will or discussed wishes for her funeral or memorial service. The adult children were afraid to bring it up, because they thought she wasn't ready to give up hope. In a separate part of the hospice with three closed doors between us and their mother, and

without the mother knowing about the meeting, we met. I spoke about how they might bring up the situation with her. They agreed to have one final dinner together that night and bring up the topic after that. I returned to this mother a short while later and her first statement to me was that she knows she's dying and she wants to bring up the topic before her kids do later that evening. She already knew!

Some people know a death has occurred even before they have been notified. This happens most often between family members who are especially close emotionally, but actually it can happen otherwise as well. I had this experience the morning that my father-in-law died.

I was four provinces away attending a two-week training, and had not spoken to him personally for six months, even though I knew from my husband that he was not well. I woke up that morning at five a.m., thought I had to use the washroom (which I never do in the middle of the night), and fell down. My legs literally collapsed under me and I dropped to the floor crushing my face into the carpet. My roommates heard me fall and asked if I was okay, and I heard myself repeat over and over – I'm okay. I'm okay. The rest of that day, I checked myself and thought I was well. At three p.m., I received a call from my husband saying my father-in-law had fallen at seven a.m. (two time zones away), gone to hospital, and died a few hours later. His fall coincided exactly with the time of my fall.

Some people can see dying people in places other than where the body lies, as if the living person separates from the body but doesn't leave this earth immediately. In most situations, this separation is not for long, and soon both disappear together.

A woman in her 70s was waiting for her own death at the residential hospice, and was visited by many of the other dying people on the night they died. She took great delight in describing the dying people in detail, even though she never left her own bed, and had no way of meeting these people. She claimed that she never saw them before they died, and they visited only within a few hours of the death, sometimes before the actual death and sometimes just after. She could describe their gender, age, and even personality traits from these short visits. She claimed that prior to coming to the hospice, on several occasions she had had premonitions about things in the future, but otherwise did not consider herself practiced in paranormal experiences.

After death, people receive "signs" that seem to come from their loved one who died (coins, feathers, birds, or movement of items). People often wonder if this is real, or just something created by loved ones to stay connected. Such stories are often quite compelling.

> I had a client come to my private practice for a single session to talk about grief. Her husband, her sister, and her dog had all died in less than three months, and she was grief stricken. In actuality, she wanted to make sure that she wasn't going crazy. She told me that she had always had a strong Catholic faith, but that her faith had been shaken with these losses. So she asked God to give her a sign. The next day she was running an errand and needed to pay for parking. She reached into her purse, (a purse she hadn't used for more than 10 years), and found a coin in the bottom of it. Before she put it in the parking meter, she looked at it. It wasn't a usual coin. It was a ceremonial coin with a picture of the Pope on it that she swears she had never seen before. And an inscription – Your husband and your sister are in heaven, and you, too, will join them one day.

Death involves a transition of energy from one form to another. It is common for electrical energy to be influenced by energy shifts around the dying process. The most common occurrence at the residential hospice is motion detector lights in the washrooms going on and off on their own without any people triggering them. Sceptics will tell you that many motion detectors are overly sensitive and may be detecting all kinds of natural movements, and that there is nothing unusual about this. But it does happen much more often in hospices than *anywhere* else I have ever worked.

> I was working at the hospice having a conversation with a new family in the hospice exactly about this problem of washroom lights. Their light was especially sensitive and the man's adult children were wondering whether there was indeed a problem or not with the lights. The gentleman in the bed told me that he was a scientist and that he thought these stories were crazy, and that of course the lighting situation meant nothing. At that moment, in front of six of us, his electric motorized bed began to move and changed from a lying down position to a sitting up position. We all stared at the electric button in full view of us all. and clearly not being touched by anyone. After a gasp, we all started to laugh. And at that, the bed went back down to its original position.

If you have been asked to be involved with someone who is dying, it may be helpful to explore your own thoughts and feelings around death before trying to be there for someone else. One place to do this is at a Death Café, as described in the first chapter. Another option might be to join a spiritual group that uses death as a regular spiritual practice. The Awaken In Toronto Buddhist Sangha and spiritual community engages the public in many such spiritual practices.[75] For the last five years, I have been hosting numerous gatherings in Toronto under their auspices. For several years, we held a Holistic Death and Dying Network for practitioners who worked in the field. This group morphed into a monthly Dying, Death, and Community group that combines both practitioners and community members interested in exploring the practical and existential issues around dying and death in Canada. We also have meditation practices specifically related to dying and death that are a part of the weekly meditation classes.

There are other such gatherings in other parts of the country. Some of these gatherings are spiritual, which others are more practical. Sarah Kerr led a group called Calgary Holistic Death Network, aimed at professionals, for many years, but that has now ended. Cassandra Yonder performs similar community deathcare services and education in Cape Breton, Nova Scotia.

Spiritual Boxes

As one gets closer to dying, it may be helpful to help the dying person create a "spiritual box" that will travel with them if them have to leave their home before they die. In this box, you can place ritual objects, copies of prayers, and written directions. Make sure everyone knows about this box, to ensure that the box goes with them, especially if they are no longer responsive and unable to remind anyone to bring it.

A Vajrayana Buddhist box will be some kind of "dharma box". Items to include can be set up as a shrine in the corner of the room. It might have some images of Amitabha, Amitayus, or Chenrezi (the archetype of compassion). It will certainly include some prayer beads. You will want copies of your Sadhanas and Bardo prayers, Loving Kindness prayers, and any other spiritual practice that you do regularly. There are other ritual items like prayer wheels, photos of your teachers, and offering bowls that will make your spiritual practice feel at home. Set up a shrine similar to the one you have in your own home. Bring reminders of nature and the life cycle, like animal bones or flowers in various states of freshness and decay.

Other forms of Buddhism have other spiritual practices for end of life. Theravada practices usually focus on the four foundations of mindfulness, especially on "the body in the body". This practice combines an awareness of not only the physical

75 Awaken In Toronto. meetup.com/AwakenInToronto

body, but also the energy body, which includes colours and vibrations. Mahayana Pureland practices teach chanting of Amitabha's name over and over. Mahayana Zen practices include chanting of the *Heart Sutra* and other prayers.

A traditional Buddhist practice called Loving Kindness Meditation is universally accepted across all forms of Buddhism. It is taught in Jon Kabat-Zinn's Mindfulness-Based Stress Reduction program, and has become the best-known end-of-life practice across people of all religions and spiritual and non-spiritual beliefs. The practice of love is truly universal, and helps put the dying person and everyone around them into a good space.

Maureen Smith, a Social Worker and Vajrayana Buddhist practitioner living in Cranbrook, British Columbia, is adept at offering the practice of loving kindness to her clients throughout their lives, as well as in her own spiritual practice.[76] There are many variations of this simple practice, and they all include generating loving kindness for self and then expanding out to others. The message of health, wellness, and happiness is expansive, and useful for holding the open space at end of life. (See Maureen's guided meditation on Loving Kindness at end of chapter.)

More than anything, the spiritual life of the dying person should be properly represented around you in a physical way to provide a familiar focus and structure. It can be easy to lose focus amidst all the changes happening. Spiritual representation helps the dying person maintain consistency between aspirations in their lives with their final wishes. Ideally you will have support from family, friends, and spiritual friends to include your spiritual wishes into your end of life wishes. If this is not the case, do your best to practice how you can.

If you are called to support a Buddhist friend who is dying, be prepared to join in with them in their specified spiritual practices. Whether those are new to you or not, try to find an open mind to give the dying person the support they want.

Multifaith Spiritual Support

If you have your own Buddhist beliefs and practices, and you are called to support a non-Buddhist at end of life, surround them with Loving Kindness practices. Loving kindness transcends all religions and spiritual practices. Never have I had Loving Kindness practices declined in any setting, as they are universal wishes for the wellbeing for all.

Use death to find the commonality of your spirituality and that of the dying person. Focus on what you have in common, not your differences. Be open to practicing their prayers and practices, even if it feels awkward to you. Above all, don't assume that everyone has a spiritual belief system. Be willing to be with people who believe only in a material world, and don't insist they take on your beliefs. It's possible to just share space together without agreeing on what's happening next.

---

76 Smith, M. *Alive Mindfully.* alivemindfully.ca

There are many supports for people who describe themselves as spiritual and who believe in "something" after death, but who don't follow a particular religion. One leader in this regard is Sarah Kerr, who is very involved in not only delivering services to families, but also in providing education to other Death Doulas or the general population about what happens at death, both just before and just after. Sarah Kerr is one such person who offers rituals and services to families, and also teaches many online courses, including one called "What Happens After We Die,"[77] that helps answer some of life's big questions. In it, she describes a map that provides a framework for understanding the ordinary and the non-ordinary experiences that happen around death and dead people. She approaches this map from a nature-based spirituality, combined with modern consciousness research. She uses inclusive language that appeals to anyone who believes that there's something mysterious going on around death.

> Nobody really knows what happens after we die; that's the nature of the Mystery. But humans are meaning-making creatures; we look for models to help understand and navigate the challenges in our lives.
>
> Each cultural and spiritual tradition has its own map of life and death, and each person has their own perspective and experiences. Some say there's nothing, some say there's something. I say there's something, and that there's a reliable map of that landscape.
>
> Dying well is easier when you have a map of how our spirits separate from our bodies, and of what happens after that. If you have a framework for understanding the non-ordinary experiences that happen around death and dead people, you can cooperate with what's happening, and the journey is much easier.
>
> *Sarah Kerr, Death Doula and Ritual Healing Practitioner*

---

77 Kerr, S. *What Happens After We Die?* soulpassages.ca

Activity 2

Loving Kindness Meditation practice[78]
By Maureen Smith, MSW, RCSW, Counsellor and Meditation Teacher

Begin by bringing awareness to your posture and sit upright and straight, so you are encouraging your body and mind to be alert, awake and relaxed. Bring your awareness to the present moment, letting go of everything that has happened up until now, this moment. And let go of thoughts about anything that may happen after this meditation is over.

Focus on the present by feeling your body in the chair you are in, by noticing the pressure on your body where it is in contact with the chair. Feel the soles of your feet on the floor. Notice the rise and fall of your abdomen as you breathe in and breathe out. Slowly allow and encourage the body and mind to slow down and be present in this moment, just as it is. There is nowhere to go. There is nothing to do. Just notice this moment of touch – feet on the floor. Body in the chair. Rise and fall of the abdomen. Breath by breath.

Now bring your attention to the place in your body in the middle of your chest between the breasts, in your heart center. Start to allow your attention to gently focus on the heart center of the body, in the middle of the chest. Notice any sensation that you may notice there.

In your heart center, start to imagine a small light in the shape of a globe, a rose, or a lotus flower. Imagine the light is the colour of a beautiful peachy-rose coloured flower petal. Let the light glow and illuminate within your heart center. Let it slowly gain strength and brightness as you breathe in. Allow your breath to flow normally.

As you exhale, notice how the lit-up rose, lotus flower, ball of light gets bigger. Now it grows to the size of a golf ball. As you breathe in, the light glows brighter, and as you breathe out, the size gets larger. A beautiful rosy-peachy coloured light expands and grows and begins to fill your chest area. Breathe in – brighter, exhale – larger. Breathe in brighter and exhale larger. As you increase the amount of light, see in your mind's eye how the light starts to fill up your entire torso.

The light glows and grows and spreads. It moves and flows through your entire torso and down into your legs, filling them up. The light expands and flows into your feet and even to the tips of your toes. The light continues to expand and flows out into your arms filling up your hands and even into the very ends of your fingertips.

Breathe in, and as you exhale, the warm light expands and flows up through your neck filling your shoulders, neck, head, face, and right up to the top of the crown of your head.

78 Clear Sky Meditation and Study Centre. *Loving Kindness Meditation Practice.*
clearskycenter.org/guided-meditations

Now you are completely full of beautiful, warm, and glowing light. Gentle, warm, and peachy-rose coloured light fills your body. Nourishing, soothing, and gracing you with loving kindness. You can say silently to yourself:

> May I be free of fear and enmity.
> May I be comfortable.
> May I be well.
> May I be at peace.

You may feel like it is all you can do to feel the loving kindness towards yourself. And if so, just stop right here and take it in. Feel the loving kindness completely envelop you, from head to toe.

But maybe you feel that you are completely filled up with bright, glowing loving kindness, and there is more energy still to share. If so, you can allow the warm nourishing light to spread beyond your body. Direct it to someone you care about and feel close to. Maybe to the person you are with who is dying. You can let the light travel from you at your heart center and imagine it flowing into them and into their heart center and filling up their body much the way the light spread and filled you up. Easefully and gently. You can wish them the same thoughts of loving kindness you wished for yourself. Silently and gently with loving kindness. You can say silently to yourself:

> May you be free of fear and enmity.
> May you be comfortable.
> May you be well.
> May you be at peace.

Allow the light and warm wishes to flow on your breath into the space around you. Allow the warm nourishing light to spread beyond your body once again. Direct it to others around you. Maybe to the people around the dying person. These may be people you get along with well, or not. Maybe you know them well, or maybe you have just met. Regardless how you feel about them, realize that sharing loving kindness with them is easy and beneficial to the dying person. Again, let the light travel from you at your heart center and imagine it flowing into the dying person, and then also into the others around. Let it flow into their heart centers and bodies. Easefully and gently. You can wish them the same thoughts of loving kindness. Silently and gently share the loving kindness. You can say silently to yourself:

> May you be free of fear and enmity.
> May you be comfortable.
> May you be well.
> May you be at peace.

When you feel it is time, allow the light to start to recede back into your body like waves on an ocean shore receding back into the ocean. Allow the loving kindness words to cease. Allow the light to come back from all people, back from the space around you. Gently and easefully bring the light back from your extremities and back into your torso. Back into your heart center. Allow the light to get smaller and smaller, dimmer and dimmer. Until there is only a tiny spark of light left. And in your heart center let that little spark of light vanish. Know that at any time you can again develop and grow this light of loving kindness within yourself. Ready to be shared with yourself and others.

7

Grief Support

Models of hospice palliative care recognize that grief involves a complex series of reactions that affect dying people and their loved ones. Hospice palliative care suggests that grief counselling be offered any time between the diagnosis phase and months (or years) after the death. Debbie Homewood, a well-known grief counsellor in private practice in York Region north of Toronto, describes grief this way – "The pain we feel when we have experienced a loss."

Grief is a feeling state connected to an emotion, which includes a basic bodily response, but added to this physiological response are the thoughts we have associated with this state. Grief includes sorrow and suffering, as well as a deep mental anguish. It also includes positive feelings like yearning and longing. It is a high-energy emotion, similar to fear with its intensity.

Normal grief is a normal reaction to a normal event. It does not need to be pathologized or avoided. Most grief will resolve with time, and not everyone needs specialized grief counselling. Grief is culturally defined and how it is expressed is also culturally determined.

There are many common losses that lead to feelings of grief: death of loved ones, death of pets, end of relationship or marriage, job layoff / termination, moving homes, ill health or aging, or loss of finances. To experience these losses is to live life. No one can avoid all of these.

The most basic principle of grief is that everyone grieves differently. Just as we are all impacted by death, there is no one right way to grieve. Grief is personal, and what works for one person might not work for another. Some people need to talk in grief, while others cry, and still others will be silent. I recognize that although I make my living today talking about death, I never attended counselling to talk about the death of my boyfriend at age 22. At that time, I just carried on, as was common for that time. Family riffs sometime occur when someone tries to make another person grieve like them, or insists that the WHOLE family does something together. This never works, and it's best to let grieving people decide for themselves what they are comfortable doing. It is not helpful to judge others' grief responses, as we are all so unique and different.

Grief plays a function in human existence. It allows us to experience some of the deeper existential emotions. The following examples demonstrate some of the different existential emotions that typically surface. Anger offers a protective defence against an unpredictable world that doesn't meet our expectations. Guilt helps us explore our culpability to let loss happen, as if we had any way to stop it. Anxiety awakens us to our lack of control of the situation. Depression allows the grieving person to turn inward and reflect on the impact of the loss. Fear is the internal alarm system that challenges our basic assumptions of self and how we relate to other. Denial shows up as an emotional anaesthesia to keep us from being completely overwhelmed.

Emotional Reactions of Grief	
Fear and Anxiety	Worry that they/others will become ill and die. Worry about family's financial situation. Worry about other family members' emotional wellbeing. Sense that the world is no longer a safe place. Etc.
Anger	Angry at the person for being sick/dying. Angry that they have to take on new responsibilities. Angry with medical professionals. Angry with peers for their lack of empathy. Anger towards previously-held belief systems. Anger towards the media for being intrusive. General sense of anger at the world. Etc.
Guilt	Regretful for things they had (or had not) said/did. Blame self for causing the illness/death. Feel as though they could have prevented the illness/death. Feel guilty for being angry at or jealous of the person who is ill. Remorseful when having fun. Etc.
Jealousy	Jealous of others who still have their mom/dad/sibling. Envious of others who had a "normal childhood." Jealous of others who have less responsibility. Jealous of the attention the dying person is getting. Etc.
Shame	Embarrassed for being different than their peers. Embarrassed to be seen with the person who is ill. Shame due to social stigma attached to the circumstances of the illness/death. Embarrassed to show emotion. Etc.
Shock	Feel emotionally numb. Quiet and disconnected. Move through the day in a daze or on "auto-pilot." Unable to absorb the reality of the loss. Etc.
Avoidance and Denial	Avoid talking or hearing about the person who is dying/has died. Avoid doing activities or going to certain places that are a painful reminder. Tell themselves it cannot be true. Block out the situation by continuing on as normal. Etc.
Withdrawal	Noticeably quiet. Keep to themselves. Don't want to go to school/work or engaged with peers as usual. Disinterested in hobbies they have previously enjoyed. Spend more time alone in their room. Reluctance to reach out for support. Etc.

There are three types of grief. The first type is anticipatory grief. This is when we experience grief in advance of the loss. We imagine ourselves in the future without the person and we feel all the feelings about that scenario. The second type is real grief in the moment of loss. This is the feeling that arises as the final breath is taken and our loved one slips away from us into death. The third type of grief is imagined grief. This is the grief about what might have happened in the future and the loss of a dream. This grief is common when parents experience the loss of a child (including miscarriages and stillbirths) or the loss of a relationship in its early stages.

People often imagine that grief is a single solitary feeling. Grief shows itself in physical, emotional, cognitive, and behavioural reactions. There are as many variations of grief as there are humans on the planet. There is no right way to "do" grief, and we cannot judge others for how they react.

Grief is first of all a physical reaction to loss. The body shows it is grieving by producing a wide variety of symptoms – headaches, nausea, appetite disturbances, shortness of breath, heart palpitations, chest pain, insomnia, or fatigue.

Grief is also an emotional reaction that triggers the most elemental of human emotions – sadness, anxiety, anger, guilt, or relief. All of these emotions, and many MORE, are normal, and may be cycled through on various days or in various situations. The Children and Youth Grief Network of Peel Region has produced a workbook that describes these various emotions well.[79] The chart below is an adapted version of their chart.

Grief also produces a large number of cognitive reactions making it hard to work or be productive when under their spell – memory problems, inability to concentrate, problems with decision making, auditory or visual hallucinations, sensing the deceased, intrusive or obsessive thoughts, or a sense of non-reality. The most common expression is brain fog, which is the sense that the brain is not working as it usually does, or at least did.

Grief causes irrational behavioural reactions in even the most rational of people – crying, wearing clothing of the deceased, keeping the room of the deceased intact (for months or even years), loss of interest in regular events, dreams about the deceased, avoiding painful reminders by avoiding locations of memories, frequent sighing, or intolerance to noise. Even though crying is the most ubiquitous symbol of grief, it can still be unsettling and even annoying if it bursts out spontaneously or for lengths of time considered to be "too long".

Most people can easily quote the DABDA model of grief accredited to Dr. Elizabeth Kübler-Ross from her *On Death and Dying* book in 1969[80] – Denial, Anger, Bargaining, Depression, Acceptance. However, in recent years, this model of grief has fallen away, as it has become clear that this model was articulated as the journey

---

79 The Children and Youth Grief Network (2018). *Handbook for Supporters – Extending Compassion and Care to Grieving Youth.*

80 Kübler-Ross, E. (1969). *On Death and Dying.*

of a dying person, but too often applied to the grieving journey. People like to think that grief is neat and tidy, and follows in a set pattern. North America jumped to follow this prescriptive plan for grief. The problem is that it's not scientific and it doesn't describe the actual grief process.

No single grief process has truly replaced her model. One simple model that many find helpful is the model set forward by Dr. William Worden, a renowned specialist on grief. He describes the grief journey as a four-part journey with specific tasks in each part. He calls it the TEAR Journey[81] –

T = To accept the reality of the loss.

E = Experience the pain of the loss.

A = Adjust to the new environment without the lost person.

R = Reinvest in the new reality.

There are few government-funded services that provide anticipatory grief counselling, but there is much to be done in the anticipatory grief stage. This is the part I feel most passionate about working with. This is the stage before the loss or death when everyone knows what is coming, but we often are reluctant to talk about it or name it. Dealing with anticipatory grief requires an orientation towards the future that is not prescriptive (not telling you what to do or feel) in what will necessarily happen, but is open to the mind's imagination. Often one resists the imagining of the loss after it happens because the mind tricks us into thinking this will make the pain worse. In actuality, leaning into the pain early makes it "easier" after the loss. Nothing will take away the pain of loss, but leaning in early can help dying people and their families make better decisions that then lead to less guilt and regret. Or sometimes the grief is experienced a bit all along the way so when the end comes, much pain has already been experienced. Anticipatory grief can be experienced by both the dying person and their loved ones, and the sharing of this experience can even make it somewhat sweet, despite the obvious sadness.

Just Show Up and Say Something

Grief makes people feel awkward. People are often unsure of what to say, and so they say nothing. Saying nothing is truly worse than saying the wrong thing. Feeling awkward is your problem, not the dying person's problem, and avoiding grief won't help anyone. As the dying person gets closer to grief, don't try to avoid it by staying away or avoiding the final moments of life. Dig deep, find supports for yourself, look around for guides to help you, and do whatever you need to do to be there for one of the most precious opportunities of your life.

---

81 Worden, J.W. (2009). *Grief Counselling and Grief Therapy: A Handbook for the Mental Health Practitioner.*

Here is a little guidance from a Kayla Moryoussef,[82] a Death Doula in Toronto, about what to say and what NOT to say involving grief and death:

1. Don't say anything that starts with "at least". Instead, just agree that it sucks.
2. Don't tell a story about someone you know who had a similar story. Keep the focus on the friend's story.
3. Don't ask "How can I help you?" Just deliver food. Or offer specific assistance.
4. Don't just say sorry. Share a story or anecdote about how the deceased person impacted you or a story you remember about them.
5. Don't ask "How are you?" Ask "How are you today?" and keep it specific.
6. Don't forget about grief after the first month. Check in on anniversaries or holidays and see how they are doing.[83]

Complicated Grief

Complicated grief is related to normal grief, but it follows after a disruption in the normal grief process. The healthy closure and healing of grief may have been inhibited and has not resolved on its own. The definition of complicated grief is culturally and spiritually determined, and what is considered complicated in one culture or spiritual community may be considered normal in another. That said, the Canadian definition of complicated is based on a medical model of grief that gets activated when complicated grief shows up in the healthcare system, most often connected to work situations.

The latest update to the Diagnostic Statistical Manual (DSM) V – the manual used by psychiatrists, doctors, and psychologists to diagnose mental illnesses – added Persistent Complex Bereavement Disorder (PSBD) in 2013. There was much debate on how to cover Complicated Grief issues. Despite this official name, regular folks still call it Complicated Grief, because that makes more sense. Of course, it's persistent and complex, but really it's complicated!

In order to qualify for a PCBP diagnosis, there are several specific requirements: There must have been a bereavement event more than 6 months before, distressing symptoms must be present every day and not just sometimes, and the symptoms cannot be better explained as depression or anxiety disorders.

There are eight types of complicated grief reactions. These are:

1. Prolonged Grief: lengthy existence of grief;
2. Absent Grief: masked, limited, or repressed grief;
3. Distorted Grief: exaggerated and bizarre behaviours;
4. Delayed Grief: numbness at first, followed eventually by intense grief;

82 Moryoussef, K. (2021). Good Death. gooddeath.ca

83 Moryoussef, K. (2021). CBC Radio. *Inappropriate Questions.* cbc.ca/radio

5. Excessive Grief: intense emotions and frightening symptoms, almost seeming psychotic;
6. Unresolved or Layered Grief: grieving a present loss but mixing it up with past unresolved losses;
7. Concomitant Grief: multiple losses close to each other making each one bigger;
8. Trauma-related Grief: mourning following horrific or violent deaths.

Each of these complications will need to be considered separately. Some are more predictable than others, and others are more dysfunctional and disruptive than others.

Common factors that complicate grief

Factors that complicate grief most often fall into the categories of personal, personality, relational, and/or emotional. Factors that fall into more than one category will intensify the reactions. Knowing that these factors exist can make us more accepting of the challenge of handing this grief:

Personal or **personality** factors are long-standing vulnerabilities related to ourselves. They include self-blame for abuse, belief that the loss was avoidable, low self-esteem, and general social problems. They can also include a history of depression or anxiety, or other mental health issues.

Relational factors are challenges in our interpersonal relationships, particularly with our families of origin. They include past challenges like childhood abuse or trauma, insecure childhood attachments, and narcissistic or overly dependent relationships. The kind of factors that trigger complicated grief are things like death of a child, uncertain death or a "Missing in Action" situation, or sudden unexpected death or loss. Ambivalence towards the loss like an ambivalent relationship with the dying person or death following a lingering illness can be two additional factors.

Emotional factors are those that involve limited capacity to feel the necessary range of feelings of grief for a variety of reasons. They include a prolonged duration of grief, a delayed or insufficient response of grief, excessive reactions, or repressed or absence of emotion. The cause for these factors may be related to unresolved previous losses, multiple losses around the same time, or an unexpressed hostility toward the loss.

Suicidal risk assessment

Whenever there has been a great loss, the treating medical team or therapist needs to listen for and ask about suicidal ideation of the loved ones grieving. A trained therapist will ask them questions about feelings of hopelessness, the possible suicide plan, mitigating factors to stop the plan, and who is around to provide support and supervision of the client. Grief must be identified as a significant risk factor in the suicide risk assessment. It is necessary to normalize grief, but not active suicidal ideation.

When suicidal ideation is active, it is critical to refer the person to other friends or family members, crisis lines, family doctors, or hospitals. If the suicidal person wants help, they can be encouraged to take themselves to a hospital emergency department for a suicide risk assessment by a psychiatrist. Everyone should know that if one is urgently worried about someone else possibly being actively suicidal, it is best to call 911 and ask for police to come to the home to take the person to hospital for a suicide risk assessment. We all need to look out for each other and to be willing to ask for professional help if we are worried about someone's state.

Grief counselling ≠ Grief therapy

Grief is a normal reaction. It is possible for family members and friends and other non-professionals to offer helpful grief counselling. Grief counselling helps facilitate uncomplicated grief to a healthy completion of the tasks of grieving within a reasonable time frame. Many hospices and non-profit agencies train persons who have experienced their own grief to then later offer grief counselling to others as volunteers. This model of peer support is extremely normalizing and helpful to remind everyone that grief is part of life.

Sometimes grief counselling is offered one-on-one, and sometimes it is offered in group format. Group sessions include time for sharing stories around grief, support for the feelings arising from those stories, and an encouragement to reorganize one's life when ready to carry on. The Bereaved Families of Ontario is one organization that provides extensive support groups around the province delivered by peer counsellors. Hospices often provide high-quality adult and children's grief groups taught by staff and volunteers that are not always well known to the public. These grief groups are usually provided free of charge and open to the public, and not just to families that have used their hospice services.

It has become common for funeral homes to offer free short-term grief groups. Funeral homes might seem like a strange source for grief groups, but their services are usually offered by social workers or psychotherapists contracted to deliver the services, and are not really connected to the funeral home except for promotion and for creating a good image in the community for the funeral home.

There are basic grief counselling skills that really should be taught to all human beings, as we are all in situations where we are invited to support grieving persons. Grief skills include active listening to stories around loss, normalizing the wide range of feelings that arise following a loss, and encouraging a healthy lifestyle. It may not seem like much, but just showing up to listen and not judge may be the greatest gifts we can offer our grieving friends and family.

For most people, grief counselling is all they need. However, for people with some of the complicating risk factors listed above, they will also need some grief therapy at some point in their lives. It is common to start with grief counselling and see how things go. Immediately after the death is not usually when persons will be ready to address deeper issues. If the grief reactions don't gradually subside on their own, grief therapy may be recommended. This is hard to determine until a month or more has passed and some of the disruptive symptoms of grief have not reduced on their own.

Grief therapy involves specialized techniques used to help people with abnormal or complicated grief. This is almost always delivered one-on-one by a professional, usually a social worker or psychotherapist.

EMDR (Eye Movement Desensitization Processing) psychotherapy is especially good for loss involving trauma, which uses sound, light, or touch rebalancing to release the trauma in the brain and the body. It is considered a somatic, body-based therapy that helps reduce the emotional memories associated with the factual memories.

CBT (Cognitive Behaviour Therapy) helps change the thoughts to get different behaviours, which leads to different feelings. CBT is particularly helpful if there are strong feelings of guilt and regret from decisions made around the loss.

Logotherapy is a type of talk therapy that involves searching for meaning about the loss and how this impacts one's purpose in life. Victor Frankl, author of *Man's Search for Meaning*, taught on these quests for grief following his own experience in the Holocaust death camps.

Doctors or psychiatrists may also suggest psychiatric medication support in the form of antidepressants if the grief manifests as depression, particularly if it makes it difficult to get out of bed, work, or get on with one's life.

Referrals to professionals in private practice that offer grief therapy can be found online through websites like *Psychology Today*. This site lists therapists by location, education, and speciality, such as grief. Persons with limited finances can also find grief therapy through non-profit agencies such as Family Services or other United Way-funded programs and agencies. Online grief support also abounds – www.mygrief.ca and www.kidsgrief.ca (both sponsored by the Canadian Virtual Hospice).

You might be unsure whether to mention the need for grief counselling or grief therapy. We often feel that it's not our business to comment on others' grief coping. However, when grief seems prolonged, absent, distorted, delayed, or excessive to you, you might want to bring it up. Also, if the individual is worried about their grief reactions themselves, they may signal an openness to hearing about options for outside help. An inability to work as before is another somewhat arbitrary line that might indicate the need to suggest a referral. And finally, when the grief seems to be getting worse and more intense, not better, it may be a sign that it's not going away on its own.

In addition to all the formal supports for grief, it is my personal wish that we all learn to support each other better through grief. If you know someone has lost a loved one, call them up. Invite them to talk about it. Say their loved one's name aloud. Be interested in remembering them and telling stories about their lives. Lean in to the awkwardness of not knowing if it's okay or not. Show up with small gifts of kindness. Food is always appreciated, particularly if it's easy and a comfort food. Ask how they are doing, really doing. And then ask again, later. Don't assume that once is enough. And if you offer help, offer it again. Grief can change moment by moment, so what you want one moment may not be what you want the next moment.

Encourage grieving people to lean on their spiritual friends and practices. Remind them to do their spiritual practices for support and strength. Invite spiritual friends to offer practical help as well as emotional help and conversations. Invite the help of Elders and Ancestors to assist with grieving.

The Buddhist concept of grief is centred on the law of impermanence. We remember that nothing lasts, and do not make too big a deal of the ending of this lifetime. Support friends and the spiritual community help out in terms of taking care of the business of moving on. Discourage too much outward expression of grief if it includes clinging. However, beware of "spiritual by-passing" and pretending to accept the death when really the grief gets pushed aside or down.

As important as impermanence is, it is important to find acceptance of all feelings and thoughts. They are not substantial and lasting, but should be noted and allowed to release. Feelings may last only 90 seconds without being supported by thoughts and stories, but they need to be seen and experienced. Doing the work of anticipatory loss from the moment we are born and beginning relationships helps to see the life cycle of birth, continuing, and death.

Grief flows in cycles. One week it seems to have passed, and then the next it can come back to smack us. One of the reasons for this is anniversaries or significant holidays. Dr. Teresa Rondo calls a return to grief after thinking one has moved on a "STUG" – Sudden Temporary Upsurge of Grief.[84] She normalizes being "stugged" and says it is common during the first couple of years, as one moves through the seasons. The first holiday, or the first birthday, or the first anniversary of the death will often be difficult, even if one thinks that they are generally handling the grief well. Eventually one settles into a new reality that makes these special days less upsetting, but it can help to expect some actions that seem like reversal in the grief process.

---

84 Rondo, T. (1991). *How To Go On Living When Someone You Love Dies.*

It's important to know that this upset is temporary, as the grief process continues to move forward once again.

It can help to plan ahead for these significant dates, in order to prevent being "stugged". It is recommended to externalize the loss in some way (light a candle, tell a story, say a prayer, make an online post), but to do something to show you remember and long for your loved one. You may also want to try doing the holiday in a different way, at someone else's house, or different food, or a new location. It is okay to completely cancel a holiday too, and to decide not to celebrate it.

Planning for significant dates doesn't mean one gets permission to act badly around these times. Using grief as an excuse to drink excessively, act violently, or generally be mean is not what's meant here. Rather, use the awareness of upcoming anniversary dates to book in extra support from friends who you know to be supportive (often not impacted by the loss like you), and make sure you have containment in place to limit drug and alcohol use.

Grief and Children

Pay special attention to the grief needs of the children, because they may need something for their grief that is different than the adults. Too often we think children are too young to know what's going on. We may try to keep them away from grief, as if they can't handle it. With the help of caring and well-informed adults in their life, children can experience grief in healthy ways. With the help of caring and well-informed adults in their life, children can experience grief in healthy ways.

Andrea Warnick, a specialist on children's grief who works out of Guelph, ON, suggests we "get comfortable with our discomfort" and take the lead by inviting children's questions around grief and loss.[85] Most children have basic questions that any adult can answer, provided they don't get too overcome by their own anxieties and existential dilemmas. She suggests we learn the Four C's, which are four common concerns experienced by children who are grieving:

1. Can I *Catch* it?
2. Can I *Cure* it?
3. Did I *Cause* it?
4. Who will *Care* for me?

There are many more suggestions by Andrea for how to communicate with children around dying and death on the Canadian Virtual Hospice website.[86] Andrea encourages us to use the "D" word – Death, as children do better with direct language, rather than abstract words that are difficult to understand. She suggests

---

85 Warnick, A. andreawarnick.com

86 Warnick, A. *Don't Use the 'D' Word: Exploring Myths about Children and Death*. virtualhospice.ca

using the words that describe the body (something children know well), such as the "the body stopped breathing". She also recommends preparing children for what they will see and hear, so they aren't surprised. And finally, children like to know what they can do, which is often passing the time, so be sure to bring activities for them if visiting someone in a hospital or hospice. One great idea is to read books for children on grief, with suggestions on Andrea's website.[87]

> Most parents instinctively try to protect their children from emotional pain. However, it's not possible to protect children from the reality of a family member's dying. Instead, it's more helpful to think of our role in such situations as preparing our children for a death, rather than protecting them from it. Children benefit from simple, honest and age-appropriate information about an impending death. Such information helps them feel included in this significant life event. We also foster their trust by demonstrating that we are not keeping the truth from them.
>
> *Andrea Warnick, Educator, Registered Psychotherapist,*
> *Nurse, and Thanatologist*

I set up a grief support program for children at Bethell Hospice. We created an art-based grief group for children and teens co-led by a social worker, an art therapy student, and a trained volunteer. Activities included artwork, journalling, and play-based activities teaching children the age-appropriate language of grief. Interacting with other children who had also experienced the death of a loved one was tremendously normalizing for these children who often feel their experiences are unique and make them different from others. We also provided packages of crayons and grief activities to children visiting in the hospice giving them something to do while visiting.

> One of my joys was seeing two grandchildren ages six and eight spend time daily with their dying grandmother in the hospice. They spent time snuggled in bed with her watching kids' Disney movies together. When they tired of that, they drew pictures with crayons and markers for her to put up in the room. Hours after she died, one of the young boys climbed into bed with her one last time, tears streaming down his face, and gave her a final hug. They were completely at home at the hospice and with her dying process.

---

87 Warnick, A. (n.d.). *Resources for Children – Books.* andreawarnick.com

8

Death as Opportunity

Love and Compassion

For me, the most rewarding part of working with illness, dying, and death is the openness to talking about love. As a registered social worker, I am trained to have strong boundaries between myself and my clients. This is required for client trust, and I really support and demonstrate these strong boundaries. Death teaches us to learn to love through these boundaries.

Death gives us permission to use the L word – love. It makes it okay professionally. I talk about love with dying persons and their friends and family all the time. I teach that without love, there is no sadness. That sadness is the consequence of feeling love, and that without love, we would just move on and not feel anything. We might push aside the sadness in grief, but that just means we don't want to acknowledge the love as well.

I tell people all the time not to try to find a place without sadness, as that place holds no love. Instead, get used to talking about love! Find the place in your heart to hold the love, sadness, joy, anger, comfort, relief, and any other feeling that wants to show up. Open up to the rainbow of feelings around death, rather than trying to shut them down.

Death is an intensely emotional time. You might find yourself recoiling from this intensity like it was a hot fire. But it will not burn you and it cannot destroy you. Along with the terrible and awful feelings, there are also memories and intense experiences of love and togetherness. Much is said in the dying process that would never have been said otherwise. It is an opening. A crack in the cosmic window. An opportunity to change. To move on and to let go.

Positive Death Movement

There are many people determined to help demedicalize death and make it better. For a while, people spoke about a "good death". Now we talk about making "better death decisions". We recognize that talking about a good death assumes that you are in charge of what you're planning, and the pressure to have a good death can put a lot of stress on the dying person. Instead, now let's talk about preparing and making good decisions.

There are countless decisions leading up to the final death moment, and the pacing of decisions is crucial. As I discussed earlier regarding the stopping of eating and drinking, it is important to be able to be in the moment, making the best decision for that moment, while also imagining what the next decision might be. And it helps to have a guide nearby who is knowledgeable about how to make these decisions.

I am grateful that there are people working in all areas of dying and death that seem to be on board with the positive death movement. The movement covers people working in healthcare, counselling, and body disposal It also includes young people thinking about how death decisions today impact the way they grieve their elders. It considers the long-term impact on the environment of today's decisions, and is so much more inclusive than simply accepting things the way they were.

The positive death movement means business people are getting involved in public death education as well. Mallory Greene is an example of this blended role of professional, who has integrated positive death into her death work.[88] She is a founder of a new cremation and green burials service in Toronto, and also someone who is deeply passionate about death education for the community. She blends these two roles seamlessly providing professional support and also advocating for better coordination of services and knowledge for dying people and their family.

> In my time working with families navigating death, I've found that they're eager to talk openly about their loss. They want to tell stories of their loved ones, speak candidly about grief and seek support as they navigate a new normal. It's helped me realize my vision of opening the dialogue surrounding death in Canada.
> *Mallory J. Greene, Co-founder and CEO of Eirene*

The positive death movement is filled with young visionaries who are hopeful, optimistic, and won't stop until they change the way the world experiences dying and death. They let themselves experience beauty and awe where the old generation saw fear and disgust. They talk about this shift as making death real. They urge us to bring dying and death into every-day life and to remember it at every opportunity.

> Education that is human, compassionate and transparent will be vital in shifting how we think and plan for end-of-life. I am confident that in my lifetime, we can rethink death and understand that a beautiful life deserves a beautiful ending, too. We can begin by recognizing that we do not wish to use our fear to defeat or dismiss

---

88 Eireen. eirene.ca

death. Instead, it is to turn this fear into curiosity and compassion to inspire and nudge us to develop a blueprint of our wellbeing and for our vulnerable and inevitable moment. The impact of dying well and with a sense of agency not only helps the person dying feel more empowered and content, but it also leaves a deep impact on the wellbeing of the people who are left behind. We cannot say for certain the level of satisfaction achieved by those who die on their own terms, but we may be able to infer that the answer lies in our inherent nature to be self-determined and purpose-seeking. Making death real allows us to live and thrive in our authentic story, thereby creating wellbeing and contentment.

Krittika Sharma, MDes Founder and
Creative Director of Maajhi,
Researcher and Behaviour Designer for Wellbeing

Beauty and Aesthetics

No one would guess that death earns us more beauty and aesthetic appreciation than anywhere else in the healthcare field. Hospital palliative care units are the ones with access to nature and out-of-doors. The 16ᵗʰ floor of the Princess Margaret Cancer Centre in Toronto boasts both the palliative care unit and a gorgeous outdoor rooftop patio that hosts musical concerts and has greenery and flowers. I volunteered for them in their Healing Beyond the Body program that delivered free resources like magazines and art supplies to dying people and their families on the palliative care floors. I attended noontime music concerts in the courtyard, and assisted patients to attend as well.

Residential hospices are grounded in prioritizing aesthetics in design of their buildings. They frequently include expansive ceilings, bright light, access to out-of-doors, flowers, and homemade quilts. They represent the best in homey furnishings. The Kensington Residential Hospice where I volunteered for two years is a renovated chapel from the old Doctor's Hospital. It has high ceilings and delightful stained-glass windows in the Great Room where families gather for the music therapy or to nibble the delicious goodies baked by volunteers when seeking breaks from the sadness of end of life.

Staff and volunteers in hospice palliative care make time to bring beauty to dying people, in whatever small way they can. PSWs delight in washing and combing hair, and share in intimate moments with dying people, bringing humanity and dignity to the dying process.

One morning I checked in on a 96-year-old woman who was clearly close to dying. My intention was to ask if she wanted any breakfast that morning. She was so weak she was unable to respond to me, but with hand motions, she asked me to open the top drawer of her dresser. In it I found a makeup purse, and she frantically used her hands to ask me to find her lipstick and apply it for her. I applied it as best I could, and she gave me the biggest smile ever. A few minutes later, her daughter walked in and exclaimed how normal her mom looked that morning. She died a few hours later, with a beautiful pink smile on her face and looking peaceful and serene.

Death as Opportunity

As described throughout this book, death brings an opening of time and space continuums. Appreciate these gaps. Make good use of the gaps. Remember the gaps.

Remember that we were made for this. Humans are created to experience life right up to the end. We have reason to think that we are able to experience our five senses even when we cannot respond. Much is made of the fact that the hearing sense is the last sense to go. So whisper in loved ones' ears, even if they cannot whisper back. Hold their hands and tell them of your love. Reassure them that you'll be okay without them. And then let them go.

I hope you have found this book useful. You have made it to the end, and possibly to the end of the 21 days of your loved one's life. You have released your loved one into death. I hope you feel that you have made good decisions along the way – the best decisions you could have made. And I also hope you have met good people along the way to support you in the caregiving and deathcare roles. It's not an easy time, but it is a profound journey.

As for me, when my legs fail to support my body, I will see this as the end of this lifetime. I will make the final preparations for the end. I will gather my loved ones close and say goodbye. And then I will voluntarily stop eating and drinking and allow death to swallow me up. You, too, can help someone do this.

Quick Reference
for Practical Lists

Palliative Performance Scale p. 27

100 (fully functioning) down to 0 (death) by 10s. There are five observable parameters included in the assessment:

- Degree of ambulation and walking
- Ability to do activities
- Ability to do self-care (cleaning and toileting)
- Intake of eating and drinking
- Level of consciousness

Trajectories of Dying p. 40

- Sudden death
- Terminal Illness
- Organ Failure
- Frailty

Sources of Pain p. 46

Physically: unable to get comfortable, reduced movement, decrease in energy;

Emotionally: increased irritability, depression, anger, worry, and a lack of appreciation for positive emotions also happening;

Intellectually: unable to focus or concentrate, brain fog, inability to do simple math, distracted mind;

Socially: lack of interest in others, inward focus, decreased tolerance of groups;

Spiritually: both increased or decreased interest in spirituality, depending on meaning assigned to pain.

ORRD Monitoring Steps p. 51

Observe: changes in the individual

Respond: remember what your scope and responsibility is and then respond accordingly

Report: to your supervisor/medical team/family members

Document: your observations

Caregiving Tips p. 61

- Don't assume you know everything;
- Ask open-ended questions and wait for a response;
- Demonstrate patience and forbearance, more than you ever thought necessary;
- Find compassion for self and others;
- Accept that the situation is as it is; and
- Imagine walking in others' shoes.

Psychosocial conversations p. 62

- Person outside the disease
- Care for the caregivers
- Support for friends and family
- Locating and arranging resources
- Psychosocial aspects and care at end of life
- How to support the dying

Dr. Ira Byock – 5 conversations at end of life p. 66

- Please forgive me.
- I forgive you.
- Thank you.
- I love you.
- Goodbye.

Dr. Max Chochinov – Dignity Therapy p. 67

Dignity Preserving Perspectives:

- Continuity of self
- Role preservation
- Generativity/legacy
- Maintenance of pride
- Hopefulness
- Autonomy/control
- Acceptance
- Resilience/fighting spirit

Dignity Preserving Practices:

- Living in the moment
- Maintaining normalcy
- Seeking spiritual comfort

Legacy Projects p. 68

- Writing or making video memoirs
- Writing letters to be given to loved ones in the future
- Organizing a lifetime of photos
- Making photo slideshows for memorials
- Distributing gifts (jewellery, special items)
- Managing social media posts

- Establishing a vigil routine for the final days or hours
- Setting up a spiritual shrine and chanting prayers

Heather Plett – Holding the Space p. 68

- Give people permission to trust their own intuition and wisdom.
- Give people only as much information as they can handle.
- Don't take their power away.
- Keep your own ego out of it.
- Make them feel safe enough to fail.
- Give guidance and help with humility and thoughtfulness.
- Create a container for complex emotions (fear, trauma, etc.).
- Allow them to make different decisions and to have different experiences than you would.

Typical Advanced Care Plan Questions p. 72

- What do I value most in terms of my mental and physical health?
- What would make prolonging life unacceptable for me?
- When I think about death, what are the things I worry about happening?
- If I were nearing death, what would I want to make the end more peaceful for me?
- What are the spiritual or religious beliefs that would affect my care at the end of life?

Substitute Decision-Making Hierarchy p. 74

- Court Appointed Guardian
- Attorney for Personal Care
- Representative Appointed by Consent and Capacity Board
- Spouse or Partner
- Parents or Children
- Parent with right of access only
- Siblings
- Any other relatives
- Public Guardian and trustee

Signs of Active Dying Phase p. 89

- Breathing changes
- Consciousness changes
- Skin changes
- Input/Output changes

Frank Ostaseski's Five Invitations p. 111

- Don't wait.
- Welcome everything, push away nothing.
- Bring your whole self to the experience.
- Find a place of rest in the middle of things.
- Cultivate "don't know mind."

Vajrayana Bardos p. 119
- Natural Bardo of this life
- Bardo of meditation
- Bardo of dream and sleep
- Painful Bardo of dying
- Luminous Bardo of dharmata – death
- Karmic Bardo of becoming.

Dr. William Worden's TEAR Journey p. 134
- **T** = To accept the reality of the loss.
- **E** = Experience the pain of the loss.
- **A** = Adjust to the new environment without the lost person.
- **R** = Reinvest in the new reality.

Kayla Moryoussef on what to say and what NOT to say involving grief and death: p. 135
- Don't say anything that starts with "at least". Instead, just agree that it sucks.
- Don't tell a story about someone you know who had a similar story. Keep the focus on the friend's story.
- Don't ask "How can I help you?" Just deliver food. Or offer specific assistance.
- Don't just say sorry. Share a story or anecdote about how the deceased person impacted you or a story you remember about them.
- Don't ask "How are you?" Ask "How are you today?" and keep it specific.
- Don't forget about grief after the first month. Check in on anniversaries or holidays and see how they are doing.

Andrea Warnick's Four C's on kids' grief questions p. 140
- Can I *Catch* it?
- Can I *Cure* it?
- Did I *Cause* it?
- Who will *Care* for me?

Quick Reference
for Websites and Books

Awaken In Toronto (n.d.).

Byock, I. (1997). 5 conversations for families at end of life. *Dying Well: Peace and Possibilities at the End of Life*. Riverhead Books.

Canadian Advanced Care Planning (n.d.). Advanced Care Planning documents for declaring end-of-life wishes for each province and territory.

Canadian Association for Spiritual Care (n.d.). Certification for chaplains in Canada.

Canadian Virtual Hospice (n.d.). Grief supports for adults.

Canadian Virtual Hospice (n.d.). Grief supports for children.

CBC Radio (May 12, 2016). Death Cafés Serve Up Life and Death Conversations.

Chockinov, H. M. (2011). Helping see the dying person as a person and not just a disease. *Dignity Therapy: Final Words for Final Days*. Oxford University Press.

Community Deathcare Canada (n.d.). National listing of private end-of-lie options.

Compassion & Choices (n.d.) Information about Voluntary Stopping of Eating and Drinking.

Death Café (n.d.). Global death education movement.

Douglas College (2021). End of Life Doula Program.

Duncan, D. and Pawasarat, C. (2021). What Happens to Consciousness during the Death Process.

Eireen (n.d.). Death education on cremation and green burials.

Ellison, K.P. (June 18, 2019). Reflections on being with dying people. *Wholehearted: Slow Down, Help Out, Wake Up*. Wisdom Publications.

EMDRIA (n.d.). Eye Movement Desensitization and Reprocessing: an intervention to treat trauma, including fear of death.

Emmanuel College of Victoria University in the University of Toronto (2021). Buddhist Psychotherapy and Mindfulness program at the master's level.

End of Life Doula Association (n.d.). Canadian listing of doula affiliations.

Gawanda, A. (2014). Imagining different advanced care planning scenarios. *Being Mortal: Medicine and What Matters in the End*. Metropolitan Books.

Green Burial Canada (n.d.). Listing of cemeteries that have green burial options.

Heath, Y. (2015). *Love Your Life to Death*. Marquis Publishing.

Holecek, A. (2013). Vajrayana Buddhism end-of-life practices and principles. *Preparing to Die: Practical Advice and Spiritual Wisdom from the Tibetan Spiritual Tradition*. Snow Lion.

Institute of Traditional Medicine (2021). Contemplative End of Life Care Program.

Kerr, S. (2021). What Happens After We Die?

Kings College at University of Western (n.d.). Thanatology degrees and certificates.

Kortes-Miller, K. (n.d.). Unconventional death educator, palliative care researcher, and social work professor. *Talking About Death Won't Kill You: The Essential Guide to End-of-Life Conversations*. ECW Press.

Kübler-Ross, E. (1969). 5 stages of grief – denial, anger, bargaining, depression, and acceptance. *On Death and Dying*. Simon & Schuster.

Moryoussef, K. (2021.). Planning for a good death using death doula services.

New York Zen Centre for Contemplative Care (2021). Buddhist training for people who want to volunteer with dying people.

Ostaseski, F. (March 14, 2017). Instructions on being with dying people. *The Five Invitations: Discovering What Death Can Teach Us About Living Fully*. Flatiron Books.

Plett, H. (March 11, 2015). What it means to "hold space" for people, plus eight tips on how to do it well.

Psychology Today (n.d.). Finding a social worker or psychotherapist in private practice by location and specialty.

Rondo, T. (1991). Definition of "STUG" – Sudden Temporary Upsurge of Grief. *How To Go On Living When Someone You Love Dies.* Bantam Publishing.

Sawatsky, K. (n.d.). One place to store all end-of-life information, passwords, and wishes to help loved ones find your information. *Modern Deathcare End-of-Life Planning Guide.*

Smith, C.G. (n.d.). Psychosocial research on conversations by PPS at end of life.

Smith, M. (n.d.). Mindfulness meditation and counselling.

Soul Passages (2021). Sarah Kerr's death education for death doulas and others interested in spiritualism.

The Children and Youth Grief Network (2018). *Handbook for Supporters – Extending Compassion and Care to Grieving Youth.*

Toronto Centre for Applied Buddhism (2021). Buddhist counselling education for lay persons and professionals.

Warnick, A. (n.d.). Grief counselling and education for grief and kids, including books on grief for children.

Warnick, A. (n.d.) Supporting kids and grief. *Don't Use the 'D' Word: Exploring Myths about Children and Death.*

Worden, J.W. (2009). TEAR – 4 stages of mourning. *Grief Counselling and Grief Therapy: A Handbook for the Mental Health Practitioner*. Routledge.

VICTORIA
HOSPICE

Palliative Performance Scale (PPSv2)
Version 2

PPS Level	Ambulation	Activity & Evidence of Disease	Self-Care	Intake	Conscious Level
PPS 100%	Full	Normal activity & work No evidence of disease	Full	Normal	Full
PPS 90%	Full	Normal activity & work Some evidence of disease	Full	Normal	Full
PPS 80%	Full	Normal activity *with* Effort Some evidence of disease	Full	Normal or reduced	Full
PPS 70%	Reduced	Unable Normal Job/Work Significant disease	Full	Normal or reduced	Full
PPS 60%	Reduced	Unable hobby/house work Significant disease	Occasional assistance necessary	Normal or reduced	Full or Confusion
PPS 50%	Mainly Sit/Lie	Unable to do any work Extensive disease	Considerable assistance required	Normal or reduced	Full or Confusion
PPS 40%	Mainly in Bed	Unable to do most activity Extensive disease	Mainly assistance	Normal or reduced	Full or Drowsy +/- Confusion
PPS 30%	Totally Bed Bound	Unable to do any activity Extensive disease	Total Care	Normal or reduced	Full or Drowsy +/- Confusion
PPS 20%	Totally Bed Bound	Unable to do any activity Extensive disease	Total Care	Minimal to sips	Full or Drowsy +/- Confusion
PPS 10%	Totally Bed Bound	Unable to do any activity Extensive disease	Total Care	Mouth care only	Drowsy or Coma +/- Confusion
PPS 0%	Death	-	-	-	-

Instructions for Use of PPS
(see also definition of terms, next page)

PPS scores are determined by reading horizontally at each level to find a 'best fit' for the patient which is then assigned as the PPS% score.

Begin at the left column and read downwards until the appropriate ambulation level is reached, then read across to the next column and downwards again until the activity/evidence of disease is located. These steps are repeated until all five columns are covered before assigning the actual PPS for that patient. In this way, 'leftward' columns (columns to the left of any specific column) are 'stronger' determinants and generally take precedence over others.

Example 1: A patient who spends the majority of the day sitting or lying down due to fatigue from advanced disease and requires considerable assistance to walk even for short distances but who is otherwise full conscious leave with good intake would be scored at PPS 50%.

Example 2: A patient who has become paralyzed and quadriplegic requiring total care would be PPS 30%. Although this patient may be placed in a wheelchair (and perhaps seem initially to be at 50%), the score is 30% because he or she would be otherwise totally bed bound die to the disease or complication if it were not for caregivers providing total care including lift/transfer. The patient may have normal intake and full conscious level.

Example 3: However, if the patient in example 2 was paraplegic and bed bound but still able to do some self-care such as feed themselves, then the PPS would be higher at 40 or 50% since he or she is not 'total care'.

PPS scores are in 10% increments only. Sometimes, there are several columns easily placed at one level but one or two which seem better at a higher or lower level. One then needs to make a 'best fit' decision. Choosing a 'half fit' value of PPS 45%, for example, is not correct. The combination of clinical judgement and 'leftward precedence' is used to determine whether 40% or 50% is the more accurate score for that patient.

PPS may be used for several purposes. First, it is an excellent communication tool for quickly describing a patient's current functional level. Second, it may have value in criteria for workload assessment or other measurements and comparisons. Finally, it appears to have prognostic value.

Definition of Terms for PPS

As noted below, some of the terms have similar meanings with the differences being more readily apparent as one reads horizontally across each row to find an overall 'best fit' using all five columns.

<u>Ambulation</u>: The items 'mainly sit/lie,' 'mainly in bed,' and 'totally bed bound' are clearly similar. The subtle differences are related to items in the self-care column. For example, 'totally bed bound' at PPS 30% is due to either profound weakness or paralysis such that the patient not only can't get out of bed but is also unable to do any self-care. The difference between 'sit/lie' and 'bed' is proportionate to the amount of time the patient is able to sit up vs need to lie down.

'Reduced ambulation' is located at the PPS 70% and PPS 60% level. By using the adjacent column, the reduction of ambulation is tied to inability to carry out their normal job, work occupation or some hobbies or housework activities. The person is still able to walk and transfer on their own but at PPS 60% needs occasional assistance.

<u>Activity & Extent of disease</u>: 'Some,' 'significant,' and 'extensive' disease refer to physical and investigative evidence which shows degrees of progression. For example in breast cancer, a local recurrence would imply 'some' disease, one or two metastases in the lung or bone would imply 'significant' disease, whereas multiple metastases in lung, bone, liver, brain, hypercalcemia or other major complications would be 'extensive' disease. The extent may also refer to progression of disease despite active treatments. Using PPS in AIDS, 'some' may mean the shift from HIV to AIDS, 'significant' implies progression in physical decline, new or difficult symptoms and laboratory findings with low counts. 'Extensive' refers to one or more serious complications with or without continuation of active antiretrovirals, antibiotics, etc.

The above extent of disease is also judged in context with the ability to maintain one's work and hobbies or activities. Decline in activity may mean the person still plays golf but reduces from playing 18 holes to just a par 3, or to backyard putting. People who enjoy walking will gradually reduce the distance covered, although they may continue trying, sometimes even close to death (eg. trying to walk the halls).

<u>Self-Care</u>: 'Occasional assistance' means that most of the time patients are able to transfer out of bed, walk, wash, toilet, and eat by their own means, but that on occasion (perhaps once daily or a few times weekly) they require minor assistance.

'Considerable assistance' means that regularly every day the patient needs help, usually by one person, to do some of the activities noted above. For example, the person needs help to get to the bathroom but is then able to brush his or her teeth or wash at least hands and face. Food will often need to be cut into edible sizes but the patient is then able to eat of his or her own accord.

'Mainly assistance' is a further extension of 'considerable.' Using the above example, the patient now needs help getting up but also needs assistance washing this face and shaving, but can usually eat with minimal or no help. This may fluctuate according to fatigue during the day.

'Total care' means that the patient is completely unable to eat without help, toilet, or do any self-care. Depending on the clinical situation, the patient may or may not be able to chew and swallow food once prepared and fed to him or her.

Intake: Changes in intake are quite obvious with 'normal intake' referring to the person's usual eating habits while healthy. 'Reduced' means any reduction from that and is highly variable according to the unique individual circumstances. 'Minimal' refers to very small amounts, usually pureed or liquid, which are well below nutritional sustenance.

Conscious Level: 'Full consciousness' implies full alertness and orientation with good cognitive abilities in various domains of thinking, memory, etc. 'Confusion' is used to denote presence of either delirium or dementia and is a reduced level of consciousness. IT may be mild, moderate, or severe with multiple possible etiologies. 'Drowsiness' implies either fatigue, drug side effects, delirium, or closeness to death and is sometimes included in the term stupor. 'Coma' in this context is the absence of response to verbal or physical stimuli; some reflexes may or may not remain. The depth of coma may fluctuate through a 24-hour period.

The Palliative Performance Scale version 2 (PPSv2) tool is copyright to Victoria Hospice Society and replaces the first PPS published in 1996 [J Pall Care 9(4): 26-32]. It cannot be altered or used in any way other than as intended and described here. Programs may use PPSv2 with appropriate recognition. Available in electronic PDF format by request https://victoriahospice.org/reprint-and-use-information

Correspondence should be sent to the Director of Education & Research, Victoria Hospice Society, 1952 Bay Street, Victoria, BC, V8R 1J8, Canada

Acknowledgments

There are so many people to thank for their help and support in getting this book published.

For starters, I want to thank all the clients and their families that have taught me so much about dying and death. Together we have learned what the dying process looks like, something that cannot just be studied and read about, but rather must be experienced. Occasionally, I have shared their stories fully and included their names with their permission. Mostly, I blended the various stories together to protect and honour confidentiality. For this deep experience of the practice of studying the modern 'charnel grounds' of death, I am eternally grateful.

I am also deeply appreciative of the many colleagues and professionals working alongside me in the end-of-life field who agreed to share quotations with me for this book. Their voices remind me that there are many unsung heroes working together to change the way Canadians approach death, and that, as we've been saying throughout the Covid-19 pandemic – 'we're all in this together'. This book is considerably stronger for the depth of experience of these voices.

There have been many teachers and mentors who helped me gain expertise in the hospice palliative care field. I am indebted to my various professors and teachers in the thanatology and palliative care courses I attended. I am also grateful to my Buddhist teachers, who encouraged me to study dying and death, and didn't make me feel crazy or morbid. I thank Doug Duncan Sensei and Catherine Pawasarat Sensei for teaching me about bardos and the afterlife, but also for their general teachings on impermanence and lovingkindness. I am grateful to have studied contemplative care at end of life with Sensei Koshin Paley Ellison and Sensei Robert Chodo Campbell at the New York Zen Centre for Contemplative Care.

The wholehearted support and encouragement of my publisher, John Negru, from our very first email exchange has been the necessary fuel to launch this first book effort. His understanding of the publication process and belief in the necessity of bringing these ideas to the world carried me through the many intricate steps.

I was blessed to have many offers of help from family and friends to read and provide feedback along the way. I am especially thankful to my son, Adrian Clark, who helped me create many of the images for the book. To my brother-in-law, David Clark, who edited and edited again with his fastidious attention to detail and grammar skills, thanks can't be said enough. I was much relieved by the feedback of my 'death buddy', Dr. Julie McIntyre, on the medical accuracy of the book, with corrections made in some areas. I was honoured to receive early guidance from Dave Bidini, a published book writer himself, who read my first few chapters and encouraged me to shift from self-publishing to looking for a publisher. And thanks to my friends, Brian Hay and Nancy Cooper, who allowed me to park my Tiny Home on their farm, where I wrote the book in its first draft form in the first two months of the Covid-19 pandemic.

Most of all, I appreciate the quiet and unflagging support of my husband, Richard Clark. He has attended countless discussions and events related to dying and death in support of my passion. He made room in our lives for my dance partner of death and even welcomed it into our lives, enriching our many conversations, while celebrating our shared life.